T0328658

Cambridge Elements ≡

Elements in New Religious Movements
Series Editor
Rebecca Moore
San Diego State University
Founding Editor
†James R. Lewis
Wuhan University

SATANISM

Joseph P. Laycock
Texas State University

CAMBRIDGE
UNIVERSITY PRESS

Shaftesbury Road, Cambridge CB2 8EA, United Kingdom

One Liberty Plaza, 20th Floor, New York, NY 10006, USA

477 Williamstown Road, Port Melbourne, VIC 3207, Australia

314–321, 3rd Floor, Plot 3, Splendor Forum, Jasola District Centre,
New Delhi – 110025, India

103 Penang Road, #05–06/07, Visioncrest Commercial, Singapore 238467

Cambridge University Press is part of Cambridge University Press & Assessment,
a department of the University of Cambridge.

We share the University's mission to contribute to society through the pursuit of
education, learning and research at the highest international levels of excellence.

www.cambridge.org
Information on this title: www.cambridge.org/9781009479370

DOI: 10.1017/9781009057349

First published 2024

A catalogue record for this publication is available from the British Library.

ISBN 978-1-009-47937-0 Hardback
ISBN 978-1-009-06029-5 Paperback
ISSN 2635-232X (online)
ISSN 2635-2311 (print)

Satanism

Elements in New Religious Movements

DOI: 10.1017/9781009057349
First published online: December 2024

Joseph P. Laycock
Texas State University
Author for correspondence: Joseph P. Laycock, j_l361@txstate.edu

Abstract: What is Satanism? The word has functioned as a powerful indictment of one's rivals, an expression of rebellion against authority, and sometimes as a label connoting the deliberate worship of dark, supernatural forces. This Element provides a concise overview of Satanism from its origins in early modern Europe through the present. It covers such topics as legends of the black mass, hellfire clubs, the Romantic Satanism of Lord Byron and Percy Shelley, and the expressed reverence for Satan of nineteenth-century occultists. It describes modern satanic religions including the Church of Satan, the Temple of Set, the Order of Nine Angles, The Satanic Temple, and others. It also addresses the contemporary Satanic Panic from the 1980s through QAnon. This Element should prove useful to anyone seeking to learn more about this complicated and frequently misunderstood tradition.

Keywords: Satanism, satanic, Satanic Panic, blasphemy, Anton LaVey, Church of Satan

ISBNs: 9781009479370 (HB), 9781009060295 (PB), 9781009057349 (OC)
ISSNs: 2635-232X (online), 2635-2311 (print)

Contents

1 What Is Satanism?

In 1992, supervisory special agent Kenneth Lanning of the Federal Bureau of Investigation (FBI) published a guide for law enforcement officials investigating allegations of satanic ritual abuse (SRA). The guide was published in response to conspiracy theories claiming that a highly organized group of criminal Satanists was systematically torturing and murdering children in blasphemous rituals – a conspiracy theory now remembered as the Satanic Panic. Many police departments assumed stories about satanic cults were true and began attending conferences on what they called ritualistic or satanic crime. Lanning specialized in investigating cases of child abuse and child sex rings, which definitely exist. However, his guide cautioned that labeling crimes as satanic was a distraction that hindered investigation rather than helping it. In a chapter titled "Definitions," Lanning explained he could not determine what it would even mean for a crime to be satanic because it is such a subjective category:

> It is difficult to define satanism precisely. No attempt will be made to do so here. However, it is important to realize that, for some people, any religious belief system other than their own is satanic. The Ayatollah Khomeini and Saddam Hussein referred to the United States as the "Great Satan." In the British Parliament, a Protestant leader called the Pope the anti-Christ.[1]

Lanning added that law enforcement training materials list a book called *Prepare for War* (1987) by Rebecca Brown as a reliable source about Satanism. But this book names "fortune tellers, horoscopes, fraternity oaths, vegetarianism, yoga, self-hypnosis, relaxation tapes, acupuncture, Biofeedback, fantasy role-playing games, adultery, homosexuality, pornography, judo, karate, and rock music" as manifestations of Satanism.[2] Brown's definition of Satanism is not only subjective; it is so broad as to be nearly meaningless.

Next, Lanning noted that while there are people who self-identify as Satanists, it is still difficult to make objective claims about what Satanism actually is: "Who decides exactly what 'satanists' believe? In this country, we cannot even agree on what Christians believe. . . . The criminal behavior of one person claiming belief in a religion, does not necessarily imply guilt or blame to others sharing that belief. In addition, simply claiming membership in a religion does not necessarily make you a member."[3]

Indeed, various satanic groups including the Church of Satan (CoS), the Temple of Set (ToS), the Order of Nine Angles (ONA), and The Satanic

---

[1] K. V. Lanning, "Investigator's Guide to Allegations of 'Ritual' Child Abuse" (FBI/US Department of Justice, 1992), p. 9.
[2] Ibid., p. 9.   [3] Ibid., p. 13.

Temple (TST) often accuse one another of being fake Satanists or failing to understand what true Satanism is, much as Christian denominations accuse each other of heresy. True Satanism is subjective from within as well as without.

This problem of definition is a serious obstacle for anyone attempting to understand or even to make accurate statements about Satanism. However, it is an assumption of this Element that Satanism is a meaningful category and that it is possible to make generalized claims about what Satanism is and is not. With this in mind, what is needed is an operational definition of Satanism. Religion scholar Ruben van Luijk defines Satanism as "intentional, religiously motivated veneration of Satan."[4] This is an effective operational definition and it has several features worth noting. First, and most importantly, Van Luijk's definition assumes some flexibility about how Satanists define Satan. Most Satanists do not imagine Satan in the same way that Christians do, as a fallen angel dedicated to evil and the destruction of humanity. In fact, most contemporary Satanists are nontheistic, meaning that they regard God and Satan as fictional characters, not supernatural realities. To nontheistic Satanists, the story of Satan's eternal defiance and rebellion is not literal but symbolic: it functions as an important myth that articulates their values and orients them toward the world. So-called theistic Satanists may understand Satan as a metaphysical reality – although not necessarily a god – that may or may not be evil. Whatever else Satanists may think about Satan, Satan is above all a powerful symbol of their values and ideals, and the centrality of this symbol is a prerequisite for anything to be considered as Satanism.

Second, the criterion that Satanism must be intentional disqualifies accusations of Satanism used to smear one's political or religious opponents, such as Brown's claim that vegetarianism is satanic. Even if there is a literal Satan who is pleased whenever someone eats a veggie burger, vegetarianism would still not meet this definition of Satanism unless someone is a vegetarian with the *intent* that their diet venerates Satan.

Third, while this definition excludes claims of "unintentional Satanism," it still allows for categorizing *imaginary* groups – groups that exist only in fantasies and conspiracy theories – as Satanism. During the Satanic Panic, it was alleged that cults were torturing children and sacrificing thousands of people to Satan. While no such groups actually existed, this conspiracy theory can be characterized as a claim about Satanism because the purported cultists were said to deliberately worship Satan.

---

[4] R. van Luijk, *Children of Lucifer: The Origins of Modern Religious Satanism* (New York: Oxford University Press, 2016), p. 5.

The distinction between real and imaginary Satanists is important because it appears that for most of the history of the word "Satanism," there were no actual Satanists. Van Luijk notes that the term appears for the first time in French and English in the sixteenth century during the European wars of religion. The available evidence suggests that Satanism began as an imaginary religion Christians invented to demonize their opponents. For this reason, Van Luijk suggests it is useful to think about the history of Satanism as "a continuous process of attribution and identification."[5] People like Brown have *attributed* Satanism to various people and activities. Meanwhile, people like Anton LaVey of the CoS have *identified* as Satanists. The public conversation about what Satanists are and do has changed over time and is shaped by these two forces.

While a useful starting point, Van Luijk's definition is not perfect. The criterion that Satanists venerate Satan can imply Christian notions of faith and worship that do not apply to nontheistic forms of Satanism. Per Faxneld, another Satanism scholar, simply avoids assumptions about the nature of religion by defining Satanism as "a system in which Satan is celebrated in a prominent position."[6] However, some of the groups discussed in this Element do not celebrate Satan. The ToS's mythology focuses on an Egyptian deity, yet it is a key group in discussions of modern Satanism because it splintered away from the CoS. Satanism scholar Kennet Granholm has proposed the term "post-Satanism" to describe groups such as the ToS. Furthermore, Satanism is part of a larger constellation of dark esoteric traditions that practitioners frequently refer to as the left-hand path. This term originated in Indian Tantra, which makes a distinction between *vāmamārga* (heterodox practices) and *dakṣiṇāmārga* (orthodox practices). *Vāmamārga* can be translated as "left-hand way" and beginning in the nineteenth century, Western occultists adapted this term to their own esoteric context. It is now used to refer to traditions that emphasize individuality, antinomianism, and self-deification.[7] Jesper Aagaard Petersen notes that discourse surrounding the left-hand path points toward "an emerging field of correspondence between Satanism, Paganism and ceremonial magic, borrowing from all," and that "Satan seems to have limited importance the further we move along the esoteric axis and into the 'Left Hand Path milieu.'"[8] That is, Satan shares the stage with other dark entities such as Set, Lilith, Hecate,

---

[5] R. van Luijk, "Sex, Science, and Liberty: The Resurrection of Satan in Nineteenth-Century (Counter) Culture," in P. F. and J. A. Petersen (eds.), *The Devil's Party: Satanism in Modernity* (New York: Oxford University Press, 2013), pp. 41–52 (p. 41).

[6] P. Faxneld, *Satanic Feminism: Lucifer As the Liberator of Woman in Nineteenth-Century Culture* (New York: Oxford University Press, 2017), p. 25.

[7] K. Granholm, "Embracing Others Than Satan: The Multiple Princes of Darkness in the Left-Hand Path Milieu," in J. A. Petersen (ed.), *Contemporary Religious Satanism: A Critical Anthology* (New York: Routledge, 2016), pp. 85–102.

[8] J. A. Petersen, "Contemporary Satanism," in C. Partridge, ed., *The Occult World* (New York: Routledge, 2015), pp. 396–406 (p. 402).

and Chaos. In practice, scholarship on Satanism generally proceeds in terms of historical connections and family resemblances that link ideas and movements rather than specific beliefs or practices that might constitute Satanism.

Anton LaVey and the Invention of Satanism

Until the twentieth century, the history of Satanism was almost entirely attribution, with no identification. In the imagination of early modern Christians, Satanists were people who had turned away from God and knowingly sided with a fallen angel who hates not only God, but the entire human race. As such, Satanists literally worshipped evil for the sake of evil. Any church or government that opposed Satanism was acting not only in its own interest, but in the interest of humanity, because it was combating a force of pure evil. Since the Christian religion also teaches that Satan and his followers are destined to lose their battle against God and suffer eternal punishment, it is difficult to imagine why anyone would actually be this sort of Satanist. In early modern Europe, most people who confessed to worshipping Satan did so only under torture or other forms of coercion.

For a significant number of people to willingly identify as Satanists, it was first necessary to reimagine Satan as a figure who is opposed to God, but not humanity. This reimagining occurred primarily in the early nineteenth century at the hands of Romantic writers. In poetry, plays, and novels, these figures cast God as a tyrant who used his omnipotent power to bully others. In rebelling against such a God, Satan was brave, noble, and a friend to humanity. These writers did not believe in a literal Satan, but speaking about God and Satan in these terms became a way of criticizing the power of churches and governments and championing the values of reason and liberty. The Romantics' poetic celebration of Satan was still not Satanism as defined by Van Luijk because it was not "religiously motivated veneration." But it was likely a necessary prerequisite to the development of religious Satanism.

Most scholars of Satanism accept that Satanism as a self-declared religion did not truly begin until 1966 when LaVey founded the CoS. LaVey openly and publicly declared himself a Satanist, and although he did not believe in a literal Satan, his books contain essays and rituals celebrating Satan. Van Luijk writes, "Genealogically speaking, every known Satanist group or organization in the world today derives directly or indirectly from LaVey's 1966 Church of Satan, even if they are dismissive of LaVey or choose to emphasize other real or alleged forerunners of Satanism."[9] However, other historians have suggested that various figures or movements that preceded LaVey may qualify as expressions of Satanism. As discussed in Section 3, following the Romantics came

---

[9] Van Luijk, *Children of Lucifer*, p. 305.

a series of esoteric religious movements that presented increasingly sympathetic attitudes toward Satan. At exactly what point this trend produced the first Satanist is somewhat subjective. At any rate, these were obscure groups and their influence on contemporary Satanism is minimal.

Satanism scholars Asbjørn Dyrendal, James R. Lewis, and Jesper Aagaard Petersen have suggested that self-declared Satanism is an "invented religion" – in the sense that it was consciously created in the 1960s and 1970s through a process of bricolage or combining different elements. LaVey and other early Satanists drew on the Romantics' glorification of Satan, legends of black masses and other "satanic" activity, and numerous other sources to create a new religion. Dyrendal, Lewis, and Petersen also note that the invention of Satanism is not a finished process, but remains ongoing.[10]

The Varieties of Satanic Experience

Almost as soon as the CoS was founded, numerous rival satanic groups began to emerge, as well as lone individuals who identified as Satanists. These groups shared some similarities, but they also disagreed on many points of belief and practice – including whether Satan really exists. Dyrendal, Lewis, and Petersen note that there is not just one Satanism but a range of Satanisms they call "the satanic milieu." As they put it: "Satanism is not a movement with the single voice of doctrine, but a 'milieu' with a multiplicity of debating voices. What they have in common may be as much the intentional act of declaring oneself a Satanist as any specific point of view."[11]

However, this does not mean Satanism is a meaningless category. Certain approaches to Satanism bear a family resemblance, creating distinct subregions within the satanic milieu. Petersen finds it helpful to theorize Satanism in terms of three ideal types: rational, esoteric, and reactionary.[12] Rational Satanism is nontheistic and emphasizes reason and materialism as antidotes to superstition and arbitrary authority. Both the CoS and TST can be called rational expressions of Satanism. Esoteric Satanism holds that Satan refers to some sort of metaphysical reality and often emphasizes magical ritual with the goal of personal transformation. The ToS can be located within this category. Reactionary Satanism is characterized by an oppositional orientation toward Christianity. Extreme examples of reactionary Satanism include figures like serial killer Richard Ramirez. Religion scholar J. Gordon Melton once referred to

---

[10] A. Dyrendal, J. R. Lewis, and J. A. Petersen, *The Invention of Satanism* (New York: Oxford University Press, 2015), p. 3.

[11] Ibid., p. 4.

[12] J. A. Petersen, "Introduction: Embracing Satan," in J. A. Petersen (ed.), *Contemporary Religious Satanism: A Critical Anthology* (Farnham: Ashgate, 2009), pp. 1–24 (p. 6).

Satanists like Ramirez as "sickies" to distinguish them from law-abiding groups like the CoS.[13] Reactionary Satanism would also include certain black metal bands, whose music invokes Satanism primarily as a rebuke of Christianity, as well as teenage dabblers, whose engagement with Satanism is motivated by shock value or a desire to defy authority and social norms. It should be noted that these are ideal types – categories scholars invented as a framework for comparison. As such, it is not uncommon for satanic groups to selectively utilize elements from all three types.

In addition to the three ideal types, a more recent division within the satanic milieu concerns whether Satanism is more focused on the individual or on transforming society through political action. LaVey often spoke of Satanism as a way of self-improvement and undoing damage caused by overbearing authority figures. For example, he framed ritual blasphemy as a form of deconditioning to liberate the individual from the stifling effects of socialization. Sociologist Edward Moody, a friend of LaVey and one of the first ethnographers of the CoS, described satanic rituals as "magical therapy" that helps Satanists be more confident and successful.[14] Despite its sinister appearance, by emphasizing the idea of "restoring one's authentic self," Satanism shares a common lineage with the New Age and human potential movements. Blanche Barton, a former high priestess of the CoS and the mother of LaVey's third child, acknowledges this connection in her biography of LaVey, although she claims LaVey's ideas came first. Barton explains, "Visit the 'New Age' section of your nearest bookstore. You'll see the entrepreneurs who have taken up LaVeyan ideas, slapping a more palatable name on them to their critical and financial profit."[15] Petersen has described Satanism as a "self-religion" in that it sacralizes the self, much like the human potential movement.[16]

Since 2013, TST has demanded the right to give prayers before city council meetings, erect satanic statues on government property, distribute satanic materials in public schools, and generally claim all the privileges the government affords to Christians. As the movement grew, TST congregations began

---

[13] J. G. Melton, *Encyclopedia of American Religions*, 7th ed. (New York: Thomson-Gale, 2003), p. 204.

[14] E. J. Moody, "Magical Therapy: An Anthropological Investigation of Contemporary Satanism," in I. I. Zaretsky and M. P. Leone (eds.), *Religious Movements in Contemporary America* (Princeton, NJ: Princeton University Press, 1974), pp. 355–82. Chris Mathews notes that Moody is mentioned in the original dedication page of *The Satanic Bible (Modern Satanism: Anatomy of a Radical Subculture* [Westport, CT: Praeger, 2009], p. 173).

[15] B. Barton, *The Secret Life of a Satanist: The Authorized Biography of Anton LaVey* (Los Angeles, CA: Feral House, 1990), p. 14.

[16] J. A. Petersen, "Modern Satanism: Dark Doctrines and Black Flames," in J. R. Lewis and J. A. Petersen (eds.), *Controversial New Religions* (New York: Oxford University Press, 2014), pp. 423–57 (p. 424).

campaigns to clean highways and help the homeless, in part because these actions showed they were not evil and possibly more compassionate than their Christian opponents. In my own work on TST, I have described such activity as "socially engaged Satanism" because the primary focus is on transforming society rather than transforming the self.[17]

The CoS regards TST essentially as plagiarism of its movement and has suggested that Satanists should be above politics instead of trying to force Satanism into the public square. The Satanic Temple, in turn, accuses the CoS of doing nothing aside from posting on social media. However, there are examples of the CoS weighing in on social issues and TST focusing on self-care.

In the final analysis, it is difficult to make claims about Satanism because it is not a single, stable thing but a milieu that continues to evolve as it is invented and reinvented, drawing on whatever materials are around it. Understanding Satanism therefore requires paying attention to a larger constellation of ideas and discourses as they have intersected and influenced each other over time. However, this situation is not so different from more familiar religious traditions such as Christianity, Islam, and Buddhism. These traditions also vary widely across times and cultures and cannot be neatly separated from other aspects of culture such as economics, politics, law, and art. In this sense, analyzing Satanism is not only useful for its own sake or for responding to claims of the Satanic Panic; it is also a mental exercise that can help theorize other religious traditions in a new light.

2 Imagining the Black Mass

Long before there were self-identified Satanists, European Christians spread rumors about satanic cults. These cults were said to operate in secret, often posing as respectable Christians. They performed blasphemous rituals and plotted to overthrow the social order. The most enduring of these legends concerned the black mass. This was believed to be an inversion of the Catholic mass in which a consecrated communion host was trampled upon and scorned instead of adored. Black masses were also said to involve orgies, the sacrifice of babies, asperging the congregation with urine instead of holy water, nude women serving as altars, and other practices deemed evil, blasphemous, or salacious.

While a minority of contemporary historians have suggested that black masses may have occurred before the modern period, albeit rarely, most

---

[17] J. P. Laycock, *Speak of the Devil: How the Satanic Temple Is Changing the Way We Talk about Religion* (New York: Oxford University Press, 2020).

historians assume they were entirely invented by Christians.[18] Van Luijk suggests that Satanism and the black mass were imaginary and invoked by competing churches for propaganda purposes.[19] Rumors that Satanists infiltrated communion services to steal consecrated hosts for desecration in black masses helped support the doctrine of transubstantiation, promulgated after the Fourth Lateran Council in 1215 CE, which asserted that consecrated hosts are the physical body of Christ. The logic was that Satanists would not go to such lengths to abuse the host unless they knew transubstantiation to be true. Accusations of Satanism peaked during the wars of religion that followed the Protestant Reformation, demonstrating their value in disparaging rival Christians. However, just because claims of Satanism were politically and theologically useful does not mean that early modern people did not genuinely believe there were Satanists.

Sociologists have noted that conspiracy theories about witchcraft, Satanism, and other forms of "evil ritual" often arise during periods of rapid social change. Conspiracy theories frequently claim that Satanists engage in inverted or backward versions of normal values. One function of these fantasies of inversion seems to be to shore up the idea that the current social order and its values are the way things must be and cannot be questioned or challenged.[20] But even though early stories of satanic activity were false and functioned as propaganda, they nevertheless laid the groundwork for the later invention of religious Satanism and they continue to influence the satanic milieu today. Folklorists have noted that stories have a strange way of becoming real through a process referred to as "ostension."[21] Legends of Satanism provide scripts that a variety of people have drawn upon, thus bringing these stories to life. Charlatans and entertainers began to perform black masses to sell magical services to paying customers or (more often) amuse tourists. In some cases, disturbed individuals have imitated stories of satanic atrocities in a process that David Frankfurter has called "mimetic performance of evil."[22] One example of this kind of ostension is Pazuzu Algarad (né John Alexander Lawson, 1978–2015), who murdered two people between 2010 and 2014. Algarad, who was diagnosed with severe mental illness following his arrest, named himself after a demon from the film *The Exorcist* and professed an idiosyncratic version of Satanism drawing largely from horror films and sensationalist media.

---

[18] J. G. Melton, *The Encyclopedia of Religious Phenomena* (Detroit, MI: Visible Ink, 2008), p. 38.
[19] Van Luijk, *Children of Lucifer*, pp. 43–5.
[20] N. Ben-Yehuda, *Deviance and Moral Boundaries: Witchcraft, the Occult, Science Fiction, Deviant Sciences, and Scientists* (Chicago, IL: University of Chicago Press, 1985); D. Frankfurter, *Evil Incarnate: Rumors of Demonic Conspiracy and Satanic Abuse in History* (Princeton, NJ: Princeton University Press, 2006).
[21] B. Ellis, *Aliens, Ghosts, and Cults: Legends We Live* (Jackson: University Press of Mississippi, 2003).
[22] Frankfurter, *Evil Incarnate*, p. 176.

Figures such as LaVey also drew on satanic conspiracy theories and imagery associated with the black mass, but in a more deliberate and creative fashion. LaVey understood that stories of black masses were merely legends, but he saw in them the potential for new religious rituals that celebrated individual autonomy and defiance of religious authorities. He kept elements of the legend that seemed interesting or fun and discarded those that seemed dangerous or pointless. In this way, rumors of satanic activity set the stage for the eventual rise of self-identified Satanism.

The Affair of the Poisons

The episode remembered as the Affair of the Poisons occurred in France during the reign of King Louis XIV between 1677 and 1682. Several prominent members of the aristocracy were accused of witchcraft or poisoning – understood at the time to be closely related practices. In total, thirty-six people were executed. The details of their confessions were printed in the gazettes, further popularizing satanic conspiracies. The Affair was certainly an example of a panic over rumors of Satanism. It is also possible that some of those accused were practicing a form of proto-Satanism.

Paris was home to a sizable class of fortune-tellers and diviners whose services included selling aphrodisiacs and providing abortions. Some were also assumed to sell poisons. In February 1677, a fortune-teller named Magdelaine de La Grange was arrested on charges of murder. Pleading for her life, she claimed to have information about other crimes and conspiracies. The claims reached the king, and the Paris chief of police was ordered to root out poisoners. Police began arresting fortune-tellers and, under torture, several of them offered up lists of clients who had allegedly purchased poison to murder their spouses or rivals in the court. Each new arrest offered the names of more potential suspects to authorities, eventually necessitating the creation of a special court called the Chambre Ardente (Burning Chamber).

In 1679, authorities arrested a fortune-teller named Catherine Deshayes Monvoisin, better known as La Voisin. La Voisin also worked as a beautician and abortionist and was said to have several members of the aristocracy as clients. An astrologer named Lesage claimed that La Voisin hosted a mass in her home where a priest named Davot performed mass over a woman's abdomen. Davot then copulated with the woman and kissed her "shameful parts" while saying mass.[23] This may be the first report of a satanic mass using a woman as an altar. La Voisin was burned at the stake in 1680.

---

[23] Van Luijk, *Children of Lucifer*, p. 46.

Next, La Voisin's twenty-one-year-old daughter, Marie Montvoisin, was brought in for questioning. She implicated an elderly priest named Étienne Guibourg as another accomplice of her mother. Marie claimed the two organized strange masses for clients said over women's abdomens. Furthermore, the king's mistress Françoise Athénaïs, Marquise de Montespan, was one such client. She feared losing the king's favor and sought help through La Voisin's magic. Marie claimed she had seen Montespan strip naked and serve as an altar. Marie also said she had seen Guibourg slit a baby's throat, pour the blood into a chalice, consecrate it along with the host, and offer it as a sacrifice to the demons Astaroth and Asmodeus. Guibourg eventually admitted to doing these things. He also claimed he saw another of the king's mistresses fill a chalice with her menstrual blood, which was mixed with bat blood, flour, and the semen of an Englishman. This concoction, it was claimed, was intended as a poison with which to murder the king. The king shut down the Chambre Ardente after his mistress was mentioned in the confessions and the Affair of the Poisons wound down. Guibourg and Marie Monvoisin were spared execution and were instead chained to a dungeon wall for the rest of their lives.

It is difficult to interpret these accounts. One possibility is that none of these masses ever took place and that these confessions were essentially sexual fantasies elicited under torture. It is also possible La Voisin was engaging in some sort of magical practice. If wealthy clients expected La Voisin to know how to invoke demons and were willing pay for such services, she could have thrown a ritual together to oblige them, making these rituals a form of ostension. Van Luijk argues that, whatever happened, the events described are not, strictly speaking, a black mass. No one confessed to adoring Satan or condemning Christ. Rather, these rituals resemble "an odd mixture of classic necromancy, alternative Eucharistic devotion, and sexual magic of unclear origin."[24] LaVey wrote about La Voisin in *The Satanic Bible*, calling her activities "organized fraud" that "stifled the majesty of Satanism for many years to come."[25] But contemporary Satanists note that subversive figures like La Voisin were the only ones who could provide abortions and remember the Affair of the Poisons as foreshadowing the connection between Satanism and the defense of reproductive rights.[26]

Lá-Bas

Paris continued to be the epicenter for speculation over satanic conspiracies and the black mass. In 1891, novelist Joris-Karl Huysmans published his novel *Lá-Bas*. Huysmans's protagonist, Durtal, is also a Parisian novelist who has grown

---

[24] Ibid., p. 53.   [25] Anton S. LaVey, *The Satanic Bible* (New York: Avon, 1969), p. 102.
[26] La Carmina, *The Little Book of Satanism: A Guide to Satanic History, Culture, and Wisdom* (Berkeley, CA: Ulysses Press, 2022), p. 61.

depressed with the spiritual emptiness of the modern world. He begins exploring Paris's occult underground in search of a satanic mass. He gets his wish and the tale ends with a detailed and graphic description of a black mass. A fallen priest named Canon Docre performs the miracle of transubstantiation, curses God, and then throws the consecrated bread to a congregation of prostitutes and homosexuals. The congregation defiles the host and a wild orgy ensues. Durtal leaves shaken, but his experience persuades him that the doctrine of transubstantiation may be true.

It was rumored that *Lá-Bas* was not fiction but autobiographical, and that Huysmans really had discovered a satanic cult active in Paris. However, there is no evidence to support this claim. In a letter to a friend, dated 1890, Huymans wrote, "I am plunged in work in search of a demonical and sodomizing priest who says black Masses. I need him for my book. I had to penetrate the world of the occultists for all that – such a bunch of simpletons and swindlers!"[27] Either way, LaVey admitted to creatively borrowing from *Lá-Bas*.[28] The Satanic Temple also drew upon this text for designing its rituals.

The Taxil Hoax

In 1892, another Parisian calling himself Léo Taxil (a pseudonym of Marie Joseph Gabriel Antoine Jogand-Pagés) began publishing his multivolume book *The Devil in the Nineteenth Century*. This was an elaborate hoax published in serial form with the help of several accomplices. It described the adventures of Dr. Bataille, a surgeon serving in the French merchant navy. Bataille infiltrated the Freemasons and his travels allowed him to witness evil Masonic rituals occurring all over the world. Taxil's hoax took every religious group that French Catholics feared and arranged them into a massive super-conspiracy: Buddhists, Hindus, and Spiritualists were all conspiring with Freemasons. Taxil even worked *Lá-Bas* into this scheme, claiming that Huysmans had really encountered Satanists, but that they had been only one part of the conspiracy. The conspiracy was headed by an even more secret order within Freemasonry called the Palladists who worshipped Satan and took their orders directly from demons.

As the saga of Dr. Bataille unfolded, it introduced a character named Diana Vaughn, a former high priestess of Palladism who had converted to Catholicism and was in hiding from Masonic assassins. Readers became obsessed with finding Vaughn and rescuing her. On April 19, 1897, Taxil held a press conference that drew journalists from around the world. He told the audience that there was no Diana Vaughn and that this had all been an elaborate hoax meant to mock the credulity of Catholics. A photo of "Diana Vaughn" was actually his

---

[27] Van Luijk, *Children of Lucifer*, p. 175.   [28] Barton, *Secret Life of a Satanist*, p. 88.

secretary who obliged in aiding his hoax. He announced that he had come to commit "infanticide" by killing the Palladist hoax and left the building under police escort.[29]

But this was not the end of the Taxil hoax. Some believers concluded that the conspiracy had coerced Taxil into saying these things, or even that Taxil had assassinated Vaughn. The 1943 noir film *The Seventh Victim* was among the first movies to depict Satanism and a favorite of LaVey's. The Satanists in this film are Palladists. Echoing the Diana Vaughn story, a young woman has told someone about their order and their laws dictate that anyone who betrays the Palladists must die. During the Satanic Panic of the 1980s and 1990s, some claims makers continued to suggest Taxil's Palladists really existed.[30]

Additional Black Mass Legends

As may have happened with La Voisin, gossip sent the curious into seedy neighborhoods in search of Satanists performing black masses and certain enterprising people were willing to give them what they wanted. From the late nineteenth century until as recently as the 1950s, tourists visiting red-light districts could pay to see what was purported to be a genuine black mass. Some were even listed in tourist guidebooks.[31] These seem to have been little more than a form of lascivious entertainment, or as Henry T. F. Rhodes wrote in 1955, "vice dressed up in the garments of theology."[32] A silent French stag film from 1928 titled *Messe Noire: Réception et Initiation au Culte Satanique d'une Néophyte* depicts a man dressed as the devil engaged in a sadomasochistic orgy with a congregation of Satanists. It is significant that French audiences in 1928 needed no exposition – the fantasy of the black mass was sufficiently embedded into the popular consciousness for everyone to understand the premise. Gerald Gardner, the father of modern Wicca, reported that in February 1952, he was invited to see a proper black mass in Rome led by fallen priests and nuns. Unfortunately, he did not have the twenty lire on hand to pay for admission. Gardner opined, "I think it was probably a show put on for tourists, though I was assured by responsible people that it was not."[33] In 1963, Princess Irene of Greece told a British magazine that she had witnessed a black

---

[29] Van Luijk, *Children of Lucifer*, p. 216.

[30] J. R. Noblitt and P. P. Noblitt, *Cult and Ritual Abuse: Narratives, Evidence, and Healing Approaches*, 3rd ed. (Santa Barbara, CA: Praeger, 2014), p. 274.

[31] N. Schreck, *The Satanic Screen: An Illustrated Guide to the Devil in Cinema* (London: Creation, 2001), p. 15.

[32] H. T. F. Rhodes, *The Satanic Mass: A Sociological and Criminological Study*, 1st American ed. (Secaucus, NJ: Citadel Press, 1954), p. 212.

[33] G. Gardner, *Witchcraft Today* (New York: Kensington, 2004), p. 28.

mass in a Paris cellar where a black cockerel was sacrificed.[34] In 1966, a black mass was portrayed in *Mondo Freudo* – a faux documentary purporting to show sexual practices from around the world. It presented staged scenes of salacious activity curated by a dry, clinical-sounding narrator. The black mass depicted in the film was allegedly held by Puerto Rican immigrants in Manhattan and was a pastiche of European legends about Satanism and racist tropes of primitive people driven to frenzy through drumming and drugs. The narrator announced that a topless dancer featured in the scene was sacrificed to Satan after the scene ended.

Legends about black masses continue to grip the public consciousness. In 2014, TST attempted to hold a reenactment of a black mass at Harvard University under the auspices of the Harvard Extension School's cultural studies club. As nontheistic Satanists, TST members attempted to explain that the black mass was a legend created by early modern Christians that Satanists had repurposed as an expression of personal autonomy. But numerous outraged Catholics – including officials from the Archdiocese of Boston – insisted that a black mass involves the ritual abuse of a consecrated host as an expression of hatred toward God and the Church. In an article for the university newspaper titled "Hatred at Harvard," a Catholic student wrote, "Historically, black masses have involved desecrating the Eucharist, which Catholics believe is the real body of Jesus Christ, by placing it on the genitals of a naked woman, urinating on it, and slitting an infant's throat to pour blood over it."[35] Some even suggested that if TST was *not* planning on performing a host desecration, then the Satanists were not doing a real black mass. St. Paul's Catholic Church near Harvard Square stopped allowing parishioners to take communion in the hand, fearing Satanists would attempt to steal a consecrated host. In the end, Harvard persuaded TST to hold its event elsewhere as an estimated 1,500 Catholics marched to the university in protest. This incident demonstrates that the black mass legend still holds a powerful influence over the Catholic imagination, even in places such as Harvard University.

3 Satanic Sympathizers

The transition from folklore about Satanists and black masses in early modern Europe to the rise of self-declared religious Satanism was long and involved several stages. The most important shift was a reimagining of Satan as a symbol of liberty, reason, and equality, which was effected primarily by the Romantics

---

[34] A. Lyons, *The Second Coming: Satanism in America* (New York: Dodd, Mead, 1970), p. 5.
[35] A. C. Griffin and L. E. Milano, "Hatred at Harvard, *The Harvard Crimson* (May 12, 2014). www .thecrimson.com/article/2014/5/12/hatred-at-harvard.

in the nineteenth century. Esoteric writers began to express increasingly sympathetic attitudes toward Satan, adding a religious element to this rebranding. Finally, small groups performed rituals honoring Satan, often alongside other personages. It is rather subjective at what point this process produced the first Satanist or the first satanic religion, but religious Satanism could not have emerged as it did without these precursors.

Romantic Satanism

Milton's *Paradise Lost* (1667) introduced the idea of Satan as a rebel possessing noble qualities. Later, William Blake described Milton as "of the Devil's party without knowing it." English scholar Peter Schock has shown how the Enlightenment dismissed Satan, leaving the Romantics free to reimagine him in a way that reflected their own values. Anti-clericalists, including Voltaire and Charles Dupuis, argued that Satan was a character from Eastern mythology that had found its way into the Bible. In response, some theologians attempted to excise Satan from Christianity. Theologian Joseph Priestley argued that Satan is a biblical allegory for evil people and that the idea of a literal Satan was only a "priestly imposition."[36]

With fewer theologians willing to defend the traditional idea of Satan, poets and intellectuals had more room to reconceive the myth of Satan's fall from heaven. As they did so, this myth became a way of critiquing both church and state. In 1793, William Blake completed *The Marriage of Heaven and Hell*. Blake reinterpreted hell as a realm of creativity and freedom that balanced the stifling order of heaven. Van Luijk called this "the first 'Satanic Bible'" because it inverted traditional Christian attitudes toward Satan.[37]

In 1821, Percy Bisshe Shelley wrote that,

> Milton's Devil as a moral being is as far superior to his God as one who perseveres in some purpose which he has conceived to be excellent in spite of adversity and torture, is to one who in the cold security of undoubted triumph inflicts the most horrible revenge upon his enemy, not from any mistaken notion of inducing him to repent of a perseverance in enmity, but with the alleged design of exasperating him to deserve new torments.[38]

The same year, Lord Byron published his play *Cain: A Mystery*. Byron's Cain is enlightened by Lucifer and concludes that any God who would condemn all humans to death for the sins of Adam and Eve is unjust and unworthy of

---

[36] P. A. Schock, *Romantic Satanism: Myth and the Historical Moment in Blake, Shelley, and Byron* (New York: Palgrave Macmillan, 2003), pp. 13–17.

[37] Van Luijk, *Children of Lucifer*, p. 43.

[38] P. B. Shelley, *A Defense of Poetry* (Charleston, SC: BiblioLife, 2009), p. 30.

worship. Also in 1821, Robert Southey, a former mentor to Shelley, described Shelley and Byron as participating in "The Satanic School" of poetry. "For though their productions breathe the spirit of Belial in their lascivious parts, and the spirit of Moloch in those loathsome images of atrocities and horrors which they delight to represent, they are more especially characterized by a Satanic spirit of pride and audacious impiety, which still betrays the wretched feeling of hopelessness wherewith it is allied."[39] Van Luijk calls this passage "the official birth certificate of the Satanic School of Poetry."[40]

Hellfire Clubs

It is one thing to celebrate the devil in stories and poetry and another to do so in practice. One of the first moves in this direction was the so-called hellfire clubs. These were groups of elite men in England and Ireland who met to hold libertine parties and mock religion. Such clubs first formed in the seventeenth century but thrived during the Enlightenment in the eighteenth century. In 1721, George I of England issued a proclamation against such clubs, but more clubs formed afterward. By some accounts, club members engaged in anti-Christian rituals that included orgies with prostitutes dressed as nuns. But there are few reliable sources describing what actually happened in these clubs – which were only later described as hellfire clubs.

Sir Francis Dashwood, the Chancellor of the Exchequer to King George III, led a group that met at Medmenham Abbey – a former abbey he leased that could easily be reached by boat from London. Francis and his friends called themselves "The Franciscans" and their activities parodied Franciscan monks. Dashwood had the motto *Fay ce que vouldras*, or "Do what you will" inscribed over the abbey's door. This was a reference to the fictional Abbey of Thélème that French monk François Rabelais described in his satirical novels *The History of Gargantua and Pantagruel* (1532–64). Rabelais imagined a backward monastery where instead of submitting to monastic discipline, monks were encouraged to do whatever they wished. *Thelema* is Greek for "will" and Rabelais's idea of a religion built around resisting rules instead of obeying them would continue to influence the satanic milieu.

The hellfire clubs were not Satanism, although they were a product of the same Enlightenment culture that preceded Romantic Satanism. They also parodied legends of black masses and satanic cults in ways that resemble some forms of contemporary Satanism. Historian Evelyn Lord suggests club members were seeking "sensual delights, sexual pleasure, and an alternative to

---

[39] Quoted in Van Luijk, *Children of Lucifer*, p. 73.   [40] Ibid.

religion."[41] These motivations could just as easily describe early gatherings of the CoS. LaVey mentions Dashwood's club in *The Satanic Bible* and interprets the club's activities as "good dirty fun" and "psychodrama."[42]

Satan and Esotericism

In the nineteenth century, esoteric writers reimagined Satan. Éliphas Lévi (né Alphonse-Louis Constant, 1810–75) was a French occultist whose work influenced Huysmans, Charles Baudelaire, and others. Lévi dismissed Satan as a superstition, yet was also critical of the Catholic Church. His writing described a lost "true religion" that united science, religion, and politics.[43] His book *Dogme et Rituel de la Haute Magie* (1854–6) contained an illustration called *The Sacredotal Hand*. It shows a priest's hand raised in benediction, but its shadow resembles the face of the devil. The surrounding text states, "Per benedictionem [*sic*] maledictus adumbratur" – by benediction the maledicted one [the Devil] is shadowed forth. The image suggests that when we attempt to banish evil and focus only on what is deemed good, we are paradoxically inviting evil, an idea with which many contemporary Satanists would agree.[44] Another image in *Dogme et Rituel* is titled *Baphomet*. It portrays a hermaphroditic entity with a goat's head, female breasts, and angel wings. Although it resembles Satan from folklore, the image symbolizes the reconciliation of opposites and embodies Lévi's idea of true religion. Lévi's Baphomet has been repeatedly parodied and pastiched, appearing on album covers and T-shirts.

One candidate for the first Satanist is Stanislaw Przybyszewski (1868–1927), a decadent Bohemian writer born in Poland. Przybyszewski's writings suggest he believed the Satanists described in *Lá-Bas* really existed.[45] He sometimes hinted that he had attended black masses in Paris himself, although there is little evidence he engaged in any sort of satanic ritual, either alone or with others. But he is the earliest known individual to describe himself as a Satanist. More importantly, Faxneld notes that his writings outline "a fairly well developed worldview with metaphysical dimensions, where Satan was the most important symbolic figure."[46] In 1897, he published the novel *Satans Kinder* (*Satan's*

[41] Evelyn Lord, *Hellfire Clubs: Sex, Satanism and Secret Societies* (New Haven, CT: Yale University Press 2010), p. xx.

[42] LaVey, *The Satanic Bible*, p. 102.

[43] J. Strube, "The 'Baphomet' of Eliphas Lévi: Its Meaning and Historical Context," *Correspondences* 4 (2016): pp. 37–79.

[44] C. McIntosh, "Eliphas Lévi," in C. Partridge, ed., *The Occult World* (New York: Routledge, 2015), 220–31 (p. 227).

[45] M. Introvigne, *Satanism: A Social History* (Leiden: Brill, 2016), p. 231.

[46] P. Faxneld, "Witches, Anarchism, and Evolutionism: Stanislaw Przybyszewski's Fin-de-siècle Satanism and the Demonic Feminine," in P. Faxneld and J. A. Petersen (eds.), *The Devil's Party: Satanism in Modernity* (New York: Oxford University Press, 2012), 53–78 (p. 62).

Children), as well as a series of magazine articles titled *Die Synagoge des Satan* (*The Synagogue of Satan*) that were collected as a book in 1900. Przybyszewski's satanic philosophy celebrated brutal social Darwinism, the primacy of sexual lust, and anarchic nihilism. He regarded Christianity as coddling the weak and the ugly, while praising Satan as "the father of life, reproduction, progression, and the eternal return."[47]

Przybyszewski's influence was small but significant. A circle of artists formed around him who became known as Satan's Kinder. This included Czech painter and occultist Josef Váchal (1884–1969) and Polish painter Wojciech Weiss (1875–1950), who painted Przybyszewski in 1899 as Satan leading a witches' Sabbath and wrote in a letter to his parents about attempts to "propagate Satanism among the crowd."[48] German horror author Heinz Ewers (1871–1943) held public lectures between 1910 and 1925 on the topic of *Die Religion des Satan* (The Religion of Satan), inspired by Przybyszewski's writings.[49]

In 1906, Carl William Hansen (1872–1936) of Denmark told the national census that his religious affiliation was Luciferian, making him another of the first self-declared Satanists. (His wife and two children identified themselves to the census as Lutherans). Hansen was a dairy salesman by trade but had also worked as an alchemist, and he joined numerous esoteric organizations. Also in 1906, he published a thirty-page pamphlet titled *Den ny morgens gry: Verdensbygmesterens genkomst* (*The Dawn of a New Morning: The Return of the World's Master Builder*) under his pen name, Ben Kadosh. Faxneld describes this text as confusing and unstructured. It explains Kadosh's goal of spreading the cult of Satan/Lucifer (regarded as the same entity) and eventually forming a new Masonic order for such a purpose. However, Kadosh's Satan had nothing to do with traditional Christianity. Like Lévi's Baphomet, Satan for Kadosh was an esoteric symbol of a vital force that permeated the universe. Kadosh's text also discussed Hiram, the legendary architect of Solomon's Temple described in Masonic traditions and initiation. Kadosh identified Hiram with Satan, an idea not found anywhere else in Masonic lore. Faxneld suggests Kadosh may have borrowed this idea from the Taxil hoax, making it a form of ostension.

Faxneld describes Kadosh as "a somewhat laughable eccentric."[50] Kadosh does not seem to have gained many followers. His only other known writing, published in 1928, concerns esoteric Christianity and contains no openly satanic references. However, a satanic group called the Neo-Luciferian Church (NLC),

---

[47] Ibid., p. 57. [48] Introvigne, *Satanism*, p. 232. [49] Ibid.
[50] P. Faxneld, "The Strange Case of Ben Kadosh: A Luciferian Pamphlet from 1906 and Its Current Renaissance," *Aries* 11 (2011), 1–22 (p. 13).

formed in 2005, has attempted to revive Kadosh's ideas and combine them with other esoteric traditions. The NLC, which is primarily active in Denmark and Sweden, has even paid for the upkeep of Kadosh's grave. Faxneld notes that the NLC is the only satanic group with a canonical writing that is more than a century old.

British occultist Aleister Crowley (1875–1947) is sometimes mistakenly described as a Satanist. Crowley was born to a wealthy British family in Warwickshire, England. His parents were strictly religious and belonged to a conservative church called the Plymouth Brethren. When Crowley was a child, his mother called him "the Beast." Rather than being shamed by this epithet, Crowley embraced it. As an adult, he joined several important esoteric groups and spent his inheritance traveling the world and self-publishing his books and poetry. He eventually founded a religion called Thelema, built around discovering and embracing one's "True Will." Crowley's axiom "Do as thou wilt shall be the whole of the law" is a foundational idea in Thelema. Like Dashwood's hellfire club, it references Rabelais's Abbey of Thelema.

Crowley's writings make many references to Satan, including a 1913 poem titled "Hymn to Satan" that begins with the words, "I adore thee, King of Evil." But in his book *Magick* (1912–13), he wrote, "The Devil does not exist. It is a false name invented by the Black Brothers to imply a Unity in their ignorant muddle of dispersions."[51] In Crowley's writings, Satan could mean a magical way of talking about the sun and the phallus (which he understood as related), the astrological sign of Capricorn (with its phallic horn), human capacity for reason and self-determination, or various spirits that a magician could invoke to reveal the darker truths of the universe. What Satan almost never meant for Crowley was the character described in the Bible.[52] In fact, Crowley argued that the Satanists of early modern Europe were actually "sincere Christians in spirit, and inferior Christians at that, for their methods were puerile."[53] However, Crowley's theories of magick (which he spelled with a "k" to distinguish it from the illusions of stage magicians), his rejection of Christian authority and conventional morality, and his philosophy of individual empowerment have had a profound impact on the left-hand path.

LaVey's detractors accused him of stealing Crowley's ideas. Both men, after all, cultivated a sinister public image and sported shaved heads. LaVey expressed some admiration for Crowley, especially his poetry, but regarded his magic as silly. He once opined, "Those who spell 'magic' with a 'k' aren't [magic]."[54] According to LaVey's friend Swedish writer Carl Abrahamsson,

---

[51] Quoted in Introvigne, *Satanism*, p. 242.   [52] Ibid., pp. 242–3.   [53] Ibid., p. 245.
[54] A. S. LaVey, *Satan Speaks!* (Portland, OR: Feral House, 1998), p. 166.

LaVey considered Crowley a de facto Satanist, "albeit an ultra-romantic one."[55] Michael Aquino built on some of Crowley's ideas, but like LaVey, used what seemed helpful and discarded the rest. Today, some Satanists are also Thelemites and vice versa, and Crowley's ideas continue to circulate within the satanic milieu.

In 1926, a bookseller and esotericist in Berlin named Eugen Grosche (1888–1964) founded a magical order called Fraternitas Saturni. The order combined Przybyszewski's writings with a variety of magical practices, including astrology, sex magic, and drug-induced trances. Their mythology equated Christ (Chrestos) with the sun and Lucifer with the planet Saturn – the furthest of the seven classical planets. Chrestos/sun and Lucifer/Saturn formed a necessary duality. As a being associated with the threshold of the furthest planetary sphere, Lucifer was regarded by the order as a doorway to transcendence, salvation, and the realm of the dead. In a ritual known as the pseudo-Masonic Saturnic Mass, the order would invoke Satan, whom they addressed as *Ophis ho archaios*, "the ancient Serpent." The order was suppressed under the Nazis, but revived after World War II. The order still exists, with members mostly in Germany and Canada; however, its Luciferian elements are less emphasized than they were before the war.[56]

In 1930, a Russian noblewoman named Maria de Naglowska (1883–1936) founded a group in Paris called the Order of the Knights of the Golden Arrow. The other name for this group was Temple de Satan. Curiously, the group appealed to Christian millennialism and claimed to be ushering in the reign of the Holy Spirit. However, Naglowska associated the Holy Spirit with women and with a positive attitude toward the human body. Like the Fraternitas Saturni, Naglowska saw God and Satan as complementary forces of the universe. Satan represented the deconstructive force of the universe that clears the way for new growth. Naglowski spoke of herself as a priestess of Satan and claimed that initiation into the Golden Arrow could provide "Truth of the Wholesome Satanic Doctrine."[57]

Initiation involved sexual magic to manipulate the dualities of God/Satan and male/female. The final initiation involved a man surrendering to the female (the personification of the coming era of the Holy Spirit) by having intercourse with her while hanging from a gallows. The male genitals were equated with Satan and the ritual represented banishing Satan to the underworld. After this ritual

---

[55] Quoted in A. Dyrendal, "Satan and the Beast: The Influence of Aleister Crowley on Modern Satanism," in H. Bogdan and M. P. Starr (eds.), *Aleister Crowley and Western Esotericism* (New York: Oxford University Press, 2012), pp. 369–94 (p. 388).
[56] Van Luijk, *Children of Lucifer*, pp. 301–2.   [57] Ibid., p. 300.

death and resurrection, the initiate became a New Man, helping to usher in the age of the Holy Spirit.

In 1936, Naglowska left Paris suddenly. It was rumored that a celebrant had nearly asphyxiated to death during the initiation and police were investigating. Naglowska ended up in Zurich, where she died later that year, marking the end of the movement. Although Naglowska's group seems to have emphasized God more than Satan, the Golden Arrow nevertheless marked an important milestone in the evolution of Satanism in that the congregation identified itself as satanic and held rituals that were open to the public.[58]

The First Satanic Church?

The CoS, which LaVey founded in 1966, insists that it was the first organized, aboveground satanic religion. While many scholars of Satanism are inclined to agree with this assessment, this depends on whether one considers any of the proceeding groups or movements to qualify as Satanism. Two other mid-twentieth-century movements are worth mentioning on this count.

In December 1968, the *Toledo Blade* newspaper reported on a barber in Toledo, Ohio, named Herbert A. Sloane (1905–75) who led a satanic organization called either the Ophite Cultus Satanas or Our Lady of Endor Coven – after the witch described in 1 Samuel 28.[59] In addition to working as a barber, Sloane was a fortune-teller who read cards and tea leaves, sometimes calling himself Kala. His group was small and met in Sloane's bedroom behind his barbershop, which Sloane called the Dragon's Den. He was heavily influenced by Margaret Murray's book *The Witch-Cult in Western Europe* (1921) and Hans Jonas's *The Gnostic Religion* (1958). Sloane taught that the God Christians worshipped was, in fact, the Demiurge who trapped human beings in a realm of matter rather than spirit. Satan, or Sathanas, as Sloane called him, has worked to free humanity from the Demiurge and took Cain as his first priest. Sloane claimed that Sathanas appeared to him when he was three years old. Sathanas appeared again when he was twenty-five and sent him to found his new religion.[60] This story would place the beginning of Sloane's group as early as 1930. However, there is no concrete evidence of this group existing before 1968. Citing their own archival records, the CoS claims that Sloane applied to found a local CoS group in March 1968 and was rejected. They conclude that Sloane began his group after this rejection and invented a false history for it.[61] If true, this would

---

[58] Faxneld, *Satanic Feminism*, p. 35.

[59] F. Aberjonois, "Witches Reported Active in Toledo," *Toledo Blade* (December 2, 1968), p. 1.

[60] S. Roberts, *Witches U.S.A.* (New York: Dell, 1971), pp. 206–7.

[61] P. H. Gilmore, "Regarding Herbert A. Sloane and His affiliation with the Church of Satan," ChurchofSatan.com (July 22, 2018). www.churchofsatan.com/regarding-herbert-a-sloane.

certainly not be the first time an esoteric tradition created a history for itself in this fashion.

The other relevant group was known as the Process Church of the Final Judgment, or just The Process. The Process began when Robert de Grimston (né Robert Moore, b. 1935–unknown) and Mary Anne Maclean (1931–2005) met at a Scientology class in London. They married, left Scientology, and founded The Process in 1965. Process members lived in a communal home in London. In 1966, thirty members moved to an abandoned salt mine in Yucatan, Mexico, to wait out the end of the world. After a hurricane struck Yucatan, they moved to the United States and the group's mythology began to take shape. The Process taught that God and the universe had four aspects named Jehovah, Christ, Satan, and Lucifer and redeeming the world involved reuniting these four personages. By the end of the 1960s, Process members were soliciting donations on the streets of San Francisco, Los Angeles, New York, and other US cities. They wore distinctive black uniforms decorated with a large silver cross and a triangular "badge of Mendes" with a goat's head. Grimston and Maclean divorced in 1973, sending The Process into a long decline. First Satan and Christ, then Lucifer, were dropped from the group's pantheon. The last iteration of the group was the Best Friend Animal Society, an animal sanctuary in Utah.

Like the groups founded by Grosche and Naglowska, The Process honored Satan and Lucifer but were not truly satanic. Following the Manson Family murders in 1969, journalists began alleging a connection between The Process and Charles Manson. During the Satanic Panic of the 1980s, journalist Maury Terry wrote a book called *The Ultimate Evil* (1987) suggesting The Process was linked to the murders of the Manson Family in Los Angeles and David Berkowitz in New York. Terry's evidence was largely limited to the fact that The Process had a presence in both cities. However, satanic conspiracy theories have swirled around The Process ever since.[62]

It is true that the CoS is the oldest satanic religion in continual existence, and it has certainly been the most influential. For historians of this tradition, it is less important to settle the question of who developed the first satanic religion than it is to understand the gradual process by which Satan was reimagined, given metaphysical significance, and finally became the subject of religious ritual.

4 The Church of Satan

Anton Szandor LaVey (1930–97) founded the CoS in San Francisco in 1966. He soon became a minor celebrity and the CoS became the most established and influential satanic organization in the world. LaVey's Satanism combined

---

[62] Introvigne, *Satanism*, pp. 328–37.

humanism, hedonism, aspects of pop psychology and the human potential movement, and a lot of showmanship. He did not believe in a literal Satan and although he sometimes hinted at the possibility of paranormal forces not yet discovered by science, his teachings and philosophy represented the rationalist approach to Satanism.

LaVey's heyday, in which he hosted celebrities at his satanic parties and appeared on talk shows, lasted only a few years and was followed by a long decline. But his mark on the satanic milieu cannot be understated. Almost immediately, the CoS inspired numerous imitator and breakaway groups. Beyond formal satanic organizations, LaVey's influence has spread widely through his book *The Satanic Bible* and through internet forums. Even Satanists who are not formal members of the CoS sometimes describe themselves as LaVeyan Satanists if their beliefs and practices are primarily derived from LaVey.

From the Magic Circle to the Church of Satan

LaVey once confessed, "I'm one helluva liar. Most of my adult life, I've been accused of being a charlatan, a phony, an impostor. I guess that makes me about as close to what the Devil's supposed to be, as anyone. ... I lie constantly, incessantly."[63] As interesting as LaVey's life was, some of the stories he told about himself are clearly embellished and parts of his biography remain contested. LaVey was born Howard Stanton Levey on April 11, 1930, in Chicago to Michael Joseph Levey (1903–92) and Gertrude August Coultron Levey (1903–84).[64] His family moved to the San Francisco Bay Area, where his father made a successful career in the liquor trade. Howard dropped out of Tamalpais High School in Mill Valley, California, at sixteen and was largely self-educated. A talented musician from a young age, he supported himself by playing the calliope and organ in nightclubs and other venues. LaVey claimed that he worked for the Clyde Beatty circus, first handling large cats and then playing the calliope. He also said he worked as a crime photographer for the San Francisco police department. Investigative reporter Lawrence Wright found no evidence that LaVey ever worked for a circus or the San Francisco police.[65] On the other hand, LaVey did own a lion named Togare that lived with him for a time in San Francisco. He also had a lifelong interest in photography that informed his ideas about magical ritual.

---

[63] LaVey, *Satan Speaks!*, p. 101.   [64] These dates are based on Ancestry.com.
[65] L. Wright, "Sympathy for the Devil: It's Not Easy Being Evil in a World That's Gone to Hell," *Rolling Stone* 612 (1991), p. 68.

LaVey had three children by three different women. In 1951, he married fifteen-year-old Carol Lansing in Reno, Nevada. Their daughter, Karla, was born in 1952. LaVey's parents allowed the family to live in a house they owned in San Francisco that LaVey would convert into his Black House. In 1960, LaVey and Lansing divorced and he began a relationship with Diane Hegarty. The two had a common-law marriage and in 1964, LaVey and Hegarty had Zeena Galatea LaVey. Diane played an active role in running the CoS through its peak in the early 1970s. In 1971, LaVey's parents signed the house over to LaVey and Hegarty. The couple divorced in 1980 and LaVey formed a relationship with Blanche Barton, with whom he had his son Satan Xerxes Carnacki LaVey in 1993.

In the 1960s, LaVey began hosting a group of bohemians at his home, whom he entertained with lectures on occult and macabre topics, including vampires, cannibalism, and psychic abilities. His group came to be called the Magic Circle and included such notables as filmmaker Kenneth Anger (1927–2023) and science fiction writer Forrest J. Ackerman (1916–2008). He eventually opened the lectures to the public and began charging $2.50 to attend.[66] During this enterprising period of his life, LaVey was hired by a strip club called Gigi to organize an act called the Witches Sabbath featuring dancers dressed as vampires and witches. One dancer was Susan Atkins, who later became a participant in the 1969 Manson Family murders. He also taught "Witches Workshops," where students could learn magical techniques of seduction and fortune-telling.

The CoS seems to have evolved organically out of these activities, starting in 1966. The official story is that LaVey founded his church on April 30 and marked it by shaving his head and declaring 1966 *Anno Satanas*, the first year of the satanic age. April 30 is known as Walpurgisnacht in European folklore. Originally a pagan holiday to welcome spring, this date is also associated with stories of witchcraft. A catalyst for LaVey's church seems to have been an article about his lectures in a San Francisco newspaper that called him "the priest of the devil." A publicity agent named Edward Webber frequented a bar where LaVey worked and suggested LaVey capitalize on his celebrity by founding "some kind of religion." A police investigator named Jack Webb who knew LaVey from the Lost Weekend nightclub offered a similar suggestion.[67]

Working with Webber, LaVey gained the attention of the press with public satanic rituals. He performed a satanic wedding on February 1, 1967, marrying journalist John Raymond and Judith Case, a New York socialite. The wedding

---

[66] Barton, *Secret Life of a Satanist*, p. 77.
[67] Schreck, *Satanic Screen*, p. 143; Barton, *Secret Life of a Satanist*, p. 80.

attracted a lot of reporters, but was not legally binding.[68] On May 23, LaVey held a satanic baptism for his daughter Zeena. LaVey baptized her three times to maximize media coverage.[69] He also made headlines on December 11 when he held a satanic funeral for Edward D. Olsen, a naval machinist who had joined the CoS six months before dying in a car accident. A naval honor guard participated.[70]

LaVey cultivated a sinister image for himself that fueled his growing celebrity. He painted his home black to serve as the international headquarters of the CoS. There, he held parties and black masses that often featured a nude woman serving as an altar. He was sometimes seen driving a coroner's van. He also owned a 1968 Jaguar with the license plate SATAN9 and a 1966 Oldsmobile with the license plate VAMPYR.[71] In 1968, he released his first record album, *The Satanic Mass*. These activities earned him appearances on talk shows and interviews in major magazines.

Some celebrities wanted in on the fun and attention. Actress Jayne Mansfield joined and had a special black-and-pink pentagram medallion made.[72] Sammy Davis Jr. also joined for a time. He reflected on this experience:

> I read enough about it to know that they weren't Satanists, they were bullshit artists and they found an exotic way they could ball each other and have an orgy. And get stoned. It was all fun and games and dungeons and dragons and debauchery and as long as the chick was happy and wasn't really going to get anything sharper than a dildo stuck into her, I wasn't going to walk away from it.[73]

In the 1980s and 1990s, LaVey's writings attracted rock musicians, such as King Diamond and Marilyn Manson, who took Satanism's sinister aspects more seriously.

One key to LaVey's success was the high level of public interest in witchcraft and Satanism at the end of the 1960s. In 1967, Ira Levin's novel *Rosemary's Baby* about a conspiracy of satanic witches became a bestseller. When the film adaptation came out in 1968, LaVey was invited to the premiere and called it "the best ad for Satanism ever screened."[74] LaVey claimed he appeared in the film wearing an elaborate devil costume. (In truth, the devil was played by actor Clay Tanner.) *Rosemary's Baby* helped LaVey in another way: while the film was still in production, Peter Mayer of Avon Publishing approached LaVey

---

[68] Schreck, *Satanic Screen*, p. 144.   [69] Van Luijk, *Children of Lucifer*, p. 297.

[70] "Satanic Rites for Sailor," *Capital Journal* (December 12, 1967), p. 20.

[71] Federal Bureau of Investigation, "Freedom of Information Act/Privacy Acts Release – Subject: Anton LaVey." https://bit.ly/46VxhTk.

[72] Barton, *Secret Life of a Satanist*, p. 90.

[73] G. Fishgall, *Gonna Do Great Things: The Life of Sammy Davis, Jr.* (New York: Scribner, 2003), pp. 236–7.

[74] G. Baddeley, *Lucifer Rising* (London: Plexus, 1999), p. 88.

about writing something that could capitalize on the current trend in witches and Satanism. This would become *The Satanic Bible* (1969).[75]

LaVey created his book from short mimeographs circulated within the CoS and found other texts to flesh it out. He added Crowley's version of "The Enochian Keys," a text originally created by the sixteenth-century English magician John Dee. LaVey altered Crowley's text further to produce a satanic translation.[76] He also adapted material from a social Darwinist tract published in 1896 titled *Might Makes Right or The Survival of the Fittest*. The tract's author, Ragnar Redbeard, was probably Arthur Desmond of New Zealand.[77] Hegarty helped in writing and editing *The Satanic Bible*,[78] which became a bestseller, selling nearly a million copies plus translations into numerous languages.[79]

The appearance of *The Satanic Bible* may be as influential as its contents. It is a small, black paperback book with a red, inverted pentagram on the cover, stylized to look like a goat head. Hebrew script surrounding the pentagram spells the name Leviathan. This image originally appeared in French occultist Stanislas de Guaïta's 1897 text *La Clef de la Magie Noire*. Guaïta's inverted pentagram contained the words Samuel and Lilith. LaVey discovered this image in Maurice Bessy's *A Pictorial History of Magic and the Supernatural* (1964) and modified it to create the "Sigil of Baphomet" that now serves as the official logo for the CoS.[80] The book has often been deployed as a prop by people who have never actually read its contents, including teenagers seeking shock value and moral entrepreneurs claiming to have knowledge of satanic conspiracies.

LaVey's Satanism

LaVey also wrote *The Compleat Witch* (1971), *The Satanic Rituals* (1972), two essay collections – *The Devil's Notebook* (1992) and *Satan Speaks!* (1998) – and numerous essays for the CoS newsletter *The Cloven Hoof*, which later became *The Black Flame*. Taken as a whole, LaVey's writings can seem contradictory. Journalist and CoS priest Gavin Baddeley described LaVey's movement as "a bizarre beast, sustained by a web of conflicting values and concepts. It is an anti-spiritual religion; a totalitarian doctrine of freedom; a cynical romanticism; a profoundly honest scam;

---

[75] J. R. Lewis, *Legitimating New Religions* (New Brunswick, NJ: Rutgers University Press, 2003), p. 112. In LaVey's own account, the idea was put forth by Fred Goerner, a writer (*Satan Speaks!* p. 5). Goerner met LaVey through his wife, Merla Zellerbach, who was a student in a workshop for witches run by LaVey.

[76] Owen Davies, *Grimoires: A History of Magic Books* (Oxford: Oxford University Press, 2009), p. 274.

[77] Dyrendal, Lewis, and Petersen, *Invention of Satanism*, p. 75.

[78] In a 1985 settlement, LaVey agreed that Hegarty assisted in the "writing, editing, and publishing" of his books and would continue to receive 10 percent of the royalties. M. Aquino, *The Church of Satan*, vol. I, 8th ed. (Michael Aquino, 2013), pp. 900–1.

[79] Davies, *Grimoires*, p. 274.   [80] Van Luijk, *Children of Lucifer*, p. 528.

a love of life garbed in the symbols of death and fear."[81] There are several reasons for these contradictions. First, LaVey was not so much a systematic thinker as a *bricoleur* who successfully wove together an eclectic range of thinkers and tropes. *The Washington Post* dubbed him "a junkyard intellectual."[82] Second, he often seemed comfortable letting people see what they wanted to see within his system in order to have a wider appeal. Third, to make his law-abiding Satanism suitably sinister, LaVey had to temper the positive and appealing aspects of his religion with elements that seemed offensive and misanthropic. He frequently referred to the axiom "nine parts respectability to one part outrageousness," which he called "a Satanic magical formula."[83]

Contradictions aside, there are some consistent themes in LaVey's philosophy. The core of LaVeyan Satanism is summed up in *The Satanic Bible* as nine satanic statements:

1. Satan represents indulgence instead of abstinence!
2. Satan represents vital existence instead of spiritual pipe dreams!
3. Satan represents undefiled wisdom instead of hypocritical self-deceit!
4. Satan represents kindness to those who deserve it, instead of love wasted on ingrates!
5. Satan represents vengeance instead of turning the other cheek!
6. Satan represents responsibility to the responsible instead of concern for psychic vampires!
7. Satan represents man as just another animal who, because of his "divine spiritual and intellectual development," has become the most vicious animal of all!
8. Satan represents all of the so-called sins, as they all lead to physical, mental, or emotional gratification!
9. Satan has been the best friend the Church has ever had, as he has kept it in business all these years![84]

To this, LaVey added eleven satanic "Rules of the Earth," which include specific prohibitions against unwanted sexual advances and harming animals or children, and nine "Satanic sins," including pretentiousness, herd conformity, and "counterproductive pride."[85]

---

[81] Baddeley, *Lucifer Rising*, p. 67.

[82] W. Harrington, "The Devil in Anton LaVey," *The Washington Post* Magazine (February 23, 1986), p. 7.

[83] R. H. Alfred, "The Church of Satan." in J. R. Lewis and J. A. Petersen (eds.), *The Encyclopedic Sourcebook of Satanism* (Amherst, NY: Prometheus Books, 2008), pp. 478–502 (p. 485).

[84] LaVey, *The Satanic Bible*, p. 25.

[85] A. S. LaVey, "The Eleven Satanic Rules of the Earth" (1967). www.churchofsatan.com/eleven-rules-of-earth; A. S. LaVey, "The Nine Satanic Sins" (1987). www.churchofsatan.com/nine-satanic-sins.

As evidenced by these lists, LaVey's Satanism emphasizes materialism and hedonism, with a strong streak of social Darwinism and political libertarianism. LaVey explicitly advocated social stratification and opposed egalitarianism.[86] He was quite open about being influenced by Ayn Rand (1905–82). In 1970, he told *The Washington Post*, "I give them [Satanists] Ayn Rand with trappings."[87] But there was also a softer side to LaVey's Satanism. He suggested that hedonism empowered Satanists to love themselves and thereby develop the ability to love others. He was quoted as saying, "If Satanists didn't care, they wouldn't be so dark and pessimistic."[88]

In addition to a philosophy, LaVey created a series of satanic rituals with help from other CoS members. For a time, rituals were held at the Black House on a weekly basis. Generally, LaVey framed the black mass and other forms of blasphemy as psychodrama and a decompression chamber that allowed an outlet for catharsis and a way of undoing social conditioning. However, in 1960s San Francisco, there was a sense that Christianity was in decline and the traditional black mass "would be like whipping a dead horse."[89] So LaVey set his sights on blaspheming other social forces. He told one journalist that a modern form of black mass "might consist of such things as urinating on marijuana, crushing an LSD sugar cube underfoot, hanging a picture of Timothy Leary or a famous Indian guru upside down."[90]

Despite claiming to be a materialist, LaVey wrote a great deal about magic, which – echoing Crowley – he defined as "the change in situations or events in accordance with one's will, which would, using normally accepted methods, be unchangeable."[91] LaVey divided magic into lesser magic, which consists of everyday techniques for influencing or manipulating people, and greater magic, which relies on rituals that effect results by summoning intense emotions that bypass the conscious mind and impose one's will on the universe. *The Satanic Bible* offers examples of such rituals for lust (willing another to engage in sexual relations with the magician), destruction (willing harm to someone as a curse, or destroying some personal obstacle), and compassion (willing another to receive healing and protection). LaVey was ambiguous about whether any part of magic was actually supernatural or if magic is a shorthand for popular psychology. He also described magic as "a way of life."[92]

---

[86] A. S. LaVey, "Pentagonal Revisionism: A Five-Point Program" (1988). www.churchofsatan .com/pentagonal-revisionism.
[87] K. Klein, "Witches Are Back and So Are Satanists," *The Washington Post* (May 10, 1970), p. 10.
[88] Barton, *Secret Life of a Satanist*, p. 213. [89] Lyons, *The Second Coming*, p. 177.
[90] Quoted in Roberts, *Witches U.S.A.*, p. 228. [91] LaVey, *The Satanic Bible*, p. 110.
[92] Aquino, *Church of Satan*, p. 850.

The Rise and Fall of Anton LaVey

LaVey was a cinephile and particularly enjoyed the noir genre of the 1940s. One of his favorite films was *Nightmare Alley* (1947), adapted from the 1946 crime novel by William Lindsay Gresham. LaVey owned a vintage movie poster for *Nightmare Alley* and Gresham was named on the dedication page of early editions of *The Satanic Bible*.[93] *Nightmare Alley*'s protagonist, Stanton Carlisle, takes a job as a carnival roustabout and uses his position to study manipulation. From Zeena, the carnival's mentalist, he learns how to trick clients into believing he is talking to the spirits of their dead loved ones. He founds a new religion called "The Church of the Heavenly Message" and begins conning wealthy clients for donations. He buys an old house where he gives lectures on tarot and other occult topics. But Carlisle eventually makes powerful enemies, loses everything, and becomes a homeless alcoholic. He again takes a job at a carnival, this time as a sideshow geek.

LaVey seems to have modeled his career after Gresham's antihero. According to Zeena LaVey (whom LaVey apparently named after the character from the novel), LaVey felt his middle name, Stanton, signified "a magical or psychic link" with the character Stanton Carlisle.[94] He claimed he worked at a circus and often spoke in terms of "conning the rubes." Like Carlisle, he founded his own religion and even gave lectures out of a large house. It is striking, then, that LaVey's career followed a similar trajectory. While LaVey never came to as bad an end as Carlisle, his organization grew rapidly in the first five years and then experienced a long, steady decline.

Initially, the CoS made posters declaring "Satan Wants You!" a parody of army recruitment posters. The address of the Black House was printed below.[95] Members even tried leaving fake dollar bills around San Francisco with ads for the CoS printed on the back sides.[96] In 1970, LaVey told *The Washington Post* that the CoS had 7,000 members in eleven countries, including Japan and Sweden, and that several congressman and senators were members.[97] This was false, but the CoS was growing at the time. One source estimates that near its peak in 1975, the CoS had about 250 active members.[98]

As more people became interested in Satanism, local CoS groups known as grottos began forming around the country. LaVey told his friend sociologist

---

[93] Ibid., p. 17.   [94] Ibid.
[95] The Church of Satan, "Satan Wants You!" (n.d.). https://bit.ly/3Sv8npn.
[96] J. Boulware, "A Devil of a Time," *The Washington Post* (August 30, 1998). washingtonpost.com/archive/lifestyle/1998/08/30/a-devil-of-a-time/da3eea5a-1b17-46db-a8f1-3cd5821247e2.
[97] Klein, "Witches Are Back," p. 10.
[98] S. E. Flowers, *Lords of the Left-Hand Path: A History of Spiritual Dissent*, 2nd ed. (Smithville, TX: Runa-Raven Press, 1997), p. 178.

Marcello Truzzi that he hoped to have a grotto founded in every state by the end of 1971.[99] The grotto system necessitated an administration, so LaVey formed a body called the Council of Nine to assist with this. The identities of council members were kept secret and the council always functioned in an advisory capacity.[100] LaVey also created a degree system for CoS members. Each rank was entitled to wear a different colored pentagram medallion, often referred to as a Baphomet. First-degree members held the rank of apprentice. Those who passed an examination entered the second degree and took the title of witch or warlock. Those who established a grotto and passed an additional test reached the third degree and could be ordained priest or priestess. The fourth degree, magister or magistra, was reserved for leaders whose influence affected multiple grottos, somewhat like a bishop. The fifth degree, magus, was held only by LaVey himself. Despite his lack of formal education, LaVey was sometimes addressed as "doctor" in recognition of this degree.[101]

Almost immediately, LaVey was asked to arbitrate disputes between and within grottos.[102] The grottos also produced numerous schismatic groups. In 1971, Wayne West, priest of the Babylon Grotto in Detroit, defected to form the First Occultic Church of Man, taking about ten members with him. West and LaVey exchanged barbs in print with West accusing LaVey of creating derivative, laughable rituals and LaVey accusing West of financial malfeasance.[103] In February 1973, LaVey excommunicated the Stygian Grotto in Dayton, Ohio. The grotto was apparently dealing in drugs and stolen goods and one member was arrested on charges of human trafficking. The following month, the grotto's leader, John DeHaven, founded the Church of Satanic Brotherhood with help from West. The Brotherhood spread rapidly for a time, but the group reportedly dissolved in 1974 after DeHaven moved to Florida, took a job as a DJ, and announced his conversion to Christianity on the air.[104] However, DeHaven reverted to Satanism and the group has continued into the present, albeit with little public activity.[105] In 1973, a splinter group in Chicago formed Thee Satanic Church of the Orthodox Nethilum Rite, and in 1974, Thee Satanic Church splintered off from this group.[106]

---

[99] M. Truzzi, "The Occult Revival As Popular Culture: Some Random Observations on the Old and the Nouveau Witch," *Sociological Quarterly* 13.1 (1972), 16–36 (p. 27).

[100] Flowers, *Lords of the Left-Hand Path*, p. 178.   [101] Ibid.

[102] A. Lyons, *Satan Wants You: The Cult of Devil Worship in America* (New York: Mysterious Press, 1988), p. 116.

[103] H. H. Ward, "Satan Rift Centers in Detroit," *Detroit Free Press* (March 25, 1972), B11; Aquino, *Church of Satan*, pp. 556–61.

[104] Lyons, *Satan Wants You*, p. 117.

[105] S. Foertsch, "An Organizational Analysis of the Schismatic Church of Satan," *Review of Religious Research* 64 (2022), 55–76.

[106] Van Luijk, *Children of Lucifer*, p. 345.

Detroit CoS members Michael Grumbowski and John Amend formed two more groups, the Order of the Black Ram and the Shrine of the Little Mother, both of which blended Satanism with neo-Nazi mythology about the Aryan race and non-LaVeyan practices such as animal sacrifice.[107] A number of far-right groups were interested in forming an alliance with LaVey in the 1970s, reportedly including the American Nazi Party and Robert Shelton's United Klans of America. James Madole (1927–79) of the white supremacist National Renaissance Party was an enormous admirer of LaVey.[108] LaVey maintained an ambivalent relationship with these groups, formally neither endorsing nor rejecting them. He was not explicitly antisemitic and once described his heritage as "Jew-gypsy."[109] But he also seemed to find the idea of totalitarianism romantic and admired the Nazis' aesthetics. Even more likely, hinting at Nazi sympathies may have been a way to keep his image suitably sinister. A 1971 *Newsweek* article noted, "If there is anything fundamentally diabolic about LaVey, it stems more from the echoes of Nazism in his theories than from the horror-comic trappings of his cult."[110] LaVey may also have seen fascists as "rubes" that could be useful. Arthur Lyons quotes LaVey's private papers: "What does it matter anymore that I can't play baseball or don't spell too good? So what if I can't get a girl? I got my armband. You see, we are dealing with intelligence levels on which imagery and ideals are easily interchangeable."[111]

There was some effort toward establishing CoS institutions abroad. In 1971, Maarten Lamers of the Netherlands read *The Satanic Bible* and traveled to San Francisco to meet LaVey. The following year, Lamers established the first international CoS grotto, known as the Magistralis Grotto or the Kerk van Satan. In 1976, Lamers moved his operation to two connected buildings in Amsterdam's red-light district. One building housed the Kerk; the other was a club called Walpurga Abbey where patrons paid by the minute to watch Satanic "monastic sisters" masturbate on stage. Lamers declared that Walpurga Abbey was tax-exempt as the sisters were performing religious acts of sexual magic. LaVey considered revoking Lamers's charter over this controversy. In 1987, after a decade of police raids and legal battles, Walpurga Abbey was legally declared a sex club, not a religious institution, and Lamers was made to pay 10 million guilders in back taxes. Baddeley interviewed a former performer at the abbey, who insisted that her performances had been acts of sexual magic, which is "one of the highest sexual ideals for Satanists."[112]

---

[107] Lyons, *Satan Wants You*, p. 117.   [108] Ibid.

[109] L. Wright, *Saints & Sinners: Walker Railey, Jimmy Swaggart, Madalyn Murray O'Hair, Anton LaVey, Will Campbell, Matthew Fox* (New York: Knopf, 1993), p. 124.

[110] "Evil, Anyone?" *Newsweek* (August 16, 1971), p. 56.   [111] Lyons, *Satan Wants You*, p. 119.

[112] Ibid., pp. 120–1; Baddeley, *Lucifer Rising*, p. 110.

In 1972, LaVey ceased holding weekly rituals at the Black House and announced that services were to be held at the local grottos. But on September 27, 1974, he declared that all regional organization should cease and that individual members and grottos should report to the Central Grotto with only minimal contact with each other. LaVey called this move Phase IV of his master plan, although it seems unlikely any such plan existed when the CoS began organizing. LaVey explained this decision. "Unity established us as a force with which to be reckoned. Now that this force has been established, further encouragement towards ingroup activity is unnecessary."[113]

In 1975, Aquino, who had become an important leader in the CoS, left and founded the ToS. (This schism is discussed further in Section 5.) Aquino took a significant portion of the CoS leadership with him. LaVey responded that these defections were Phase V of his master plan. He observed, "These people were groupies, not Satanists. They were the kind of people who would attend a ritual, then put on their Baphomets and go out to the nearest Denny's. Big deal."[114]

That year LaVey disbanded the grotto system completely. He also painted the Black House beige to reduce unwanted attention and largely retired from public life.[115] This move meant that for most members, the CoS consisted of little more than receiving a newsletter.[116] The CoS leadership insists that LaVey did not give up, but rather turned the CoS into what it was always meant to be: an exclusive club for "the alien elite." Barton explained, "LaVey wanted his Church of Satan to evolve into a truly cabalistic underground rather than degenerating into a long-running public pageant or a 'Satan pen pal club.'"[117] Accordingly, "Satan Wants You!" was replaced with a parody of the marines' recruitment slogan "We're looking for a few good men."

Master plans aside, Lewis concluded that LaVey "was not up to making the necessary personal sacrifices that being a founding prophet and leader required because his pecuniary and self-aggrandizing motives for forming CoS were so shallow."[118] In 2020, the FBI released a report on an investigation of LaVey conducted in 1980 after a disturbed informant in Chicago claimed LaVey was orchestrating a plot to assassinate Senator Ted Kennedy. The San Francisco Police Department informed the FBI that LaVey was "not personally active in the Church of Satan, having become disillusioned and now devotes his time to writing books." FBI agents interviewed LaVey in his home on October 31. They

---

[113] Aquino, *Church of Satan*, p. 794.   [114] Lyons, *Satan Wants You*, p. 118.

[115] Van Luijk, *Children of Lucifer*, p. 363.

[116] P. Faxneld and J. A. Petersen, "Part Two: The Black Pope and the Church of Satan," in P. Faxneld and J. A. Petersen (eds.), *The Devil's Party: Satanism in Modernity* (New York: Oxford University Press, 2013), pp. 80–3 (p. 81).

[117] Barton, *Secret Life of a Satanist*, p. 115.   [118] Lewis, *Legitimating New Religions*, p. 111.

reported: "LAVEY STATED THAT HE IS WELL AWARE THAT MOST PEOPLE ASSOCIATED WITH THE CHURCH OF SATAN ARE IN FACT 'FANATICS, CULTISTS, AND WEIRDOES.' HE STATED HIS INTEREST IN THE CHURCH OF SATAN IS STRICTLY FROM A MONETARY POINT OF VIEW AND SPENDS HIS TIME FURNISHING INTERVIEWS, WRITING MATERIALS, AND LATELY HAS BEOME INTERESTED IN PHOTOGRAPHY."[119]

The agents left, satisfied LaVey was not a threat. LaVey was adept at telling people what they wanted to hear and might have been doing this with the FBI. But this report also supports Lewis's suspicion that LaVey painted himself into a corner where he no longer wished to lead a satanic organization but had no other opportunities to earn a living. LaVey's financial problems soon grew worse. In 1988, Hegarty filed a palimony suit against LaVey that would last for years. This too may have been a factor in his long period of silence.

The Black House was again painted black in 1986, but LaVey grew increasingly reclusive. He began sending his daughter Zeena to represent the CoS. In 1988, Zeena married prominent CoS member Nikolas Schreck and took her husband's name. By this time, a new cohort of CoS leadership was flirting with fascism more openly. On August 8, 1988, the Schrecks and CoS leader Boyd Rice organized a "Satanic rally" at the Strand Theater in San Francisco to celebrate the death of the 1960s. Afterward, Rice gave an interview sitting before a satanic altar draped in a Nazi flag and stated, "We need to bring power back to the powerful. We need the slaves to be enslaved again."[120] Petersen describes the 8-8-88 rally as "play with gray," in which Satanists intentionally blurred the boundaries between endorsing fascism and ironic play.[121] This sort of play was a logical extension of LaVey's strategy of trying to combine outrage and respectability.

On Walpurgisnacht 1990, Zeena formally renounced any association with the CoS or LaVey, whom she called her "unfather." The Schrecks joined the ToS for a time and in 2002 formed their own esoteric left-hand path group, the Sethian Liberation Movement. In 1991, Zeena testified on behalf of her mother, Diane Hegarty, against LaVey. A court awarded Hegarty half of LaVey's property, bankrupting him. That same year, Wright published an

---

[119] Federal Bureau of Investigation, "Freedom of Information Act/Privacy Acts Release – Subject: Anton LaVey," spelling and capitalization as in original.

[120] "8/8/88 Rally: Radio Werewolf, Boyd Rice, Zeena Schreck, Adam Parfrey." youtube.com/watch?v=vx0kRUOzrxI.

[121] J. A. Petersen, "'Smite Him Hip and Thigh': Satanism, Violence, and Transgression," in J. R. Lewis (ed.), *Violence and New Religious Movements* (New York: Oxford University Press, 2011), pp. 351–78 (p. 352).

article in *Rolling Stone* debunking much of LaVey's biography. Wright recalled, "Whatever it had been in the past, it certainly wasn't when I went to meet him. . . . I think he was very glad to meet my expense account."[122] On May 8, 1992, Hegarty and LaVey agreed to sell the Black House for $240,000 to Donald Werby, a real estate developer who had known LaVey since the days of the Magic Circle. The proceeds were used to settle the divorce and Werby allowed LaVey to continue to live in the house for free.[123]

After a long battle with a heart condition, LaVey died in St. Mary's Hospital in San Francisco on October 29, 1997. His total assets, including book royalties, amounted to $60,000.[124] His followers wrote on his death certificate that he died on Halloween, but Zeena had the date corrected. The following year, the Schrecks produced a document called "Anton LaVey: Myth and Reality," challenging many of the claims about LaVey's biography.

On November 7, 1997, LaVey's partner, Barton, and his oldest daughter, Karla LaVey, held a press conference announcing that they would now lead the CoS as joint high priestesses. This alliance was short-lived. Barton produced a will in which LaVey made her sole trustee of the CoS until her son, Xerxes, came of age. Karla persuaded the court that this will was invalid. A settlement was reached in which Barton kept the name of the organization while LaVey's belongings and copyrights were divided among his three children. Barton was forced to leave the Black House. After a failed fundraising effort to purchase it, the house was demolished on October 16, 2001.[125]

In 1998, Wright declared, "There's no future for that church unless some other person comes along who can spin out the same kind of charisma that LaVey was able to do."[126] This prediction wasn't quite right, although the CoS never had another figure like LaVey. In 1999, Karla LaVey formed a splinter group named the First Satanic Church. The group's primary activity is an annual Christmas concert called Black X-Mass. Barton remained high priestess until 2002 and then passed this role on to Peter Gilmore and his wife, Peggy Nadramia, who ran an active group in New York. In 2007, Gilmore published *The Satanic Scriptures*, which contained original essays and previously unpublished rituals. Outside of the CoS, LaVey's influence remains significant. In addition to the countless, ephemeral satanic groups that formed using LaVey's example, the Internet became a vector where LaVey's ideas have continued to evolve and shape the satanic milieu.

---

[122] Boulware, "A Devil of a Time."   [123] Ibid.   [124] Ibid.
[125] Introvigne, *Satanism*, pp. 516–17.   [126] Boulware, "A Devil of a Time."

5 The Temple of Set and Esoteric Satanism

Whereas rationalist approaches to Satanism understand Satan as a symbol of human potential, esoteric Satanism posits that supernatural entities exist and can be influenced or communed with through ritual. While LaVey's Satanism is primarily concerned with living well, esoteric Satanism often espouses soteriological or eschatological goals. A seminal moment in modern esoteric Satanism occurred in 1975 when Michael Aquino broke with the CoS to form the ToS. The ToS influenced numerous other left-hand path groups, satanic and otherwise. Esoteric forms of Satanism are not inherently dangerous. A worldview that prioritizes transcendent realities over ordinary existence, however, combined with a desire to move away from the safe Satanism LaVey espoused, has led some forms of esoteric Satanism toward violence. The so-called sinister tradition refers to a current of esoteric Satanism that endorses human sacrifice and has been linked to extreme political movements.

The Temple of Set

In June 1968, Aquino had just graduated from the University of California at Santa Barbara and was attending the premiere of *Rosemary's Baby*. There, he spotted LaVey with a group of black-robed followers. Soon after, he traveled to Fort Bragg, North Carolina, for army training as a psychological operations specialist.[127] The following March, he returned to San Francisco to be married, saw an ad for the CoS in an underground newspaper called the *Berkeley Barb*, and attended one of LaVey's Friday night rituals.[128]

In June 1969, he began a tour of active duty in Vietnam and took with him a copy of Milton's *Paradise Lost*. Writing in a war zone, Aquino produced his own epic text, *The Diabolicon*. Within it, various demons describe how God sought to freeze the universe within an all-consuming, static pattern; Satan alone had the capacity to resist this plan, creating the possibilities of change and self-determination. Aquino sent a copy to LaVey, who saw Aquino's potential. When Aquino returned to the United States in 1971, he established the Nineveh Grotto in Louisville, Kentucky, where he was stationed. LaVey made him editor of the CoS newsletter, *The Cloven Hoof*, and by the end of the year, Aquino was appointed to the grade of magister, one rank below LaVey himself.

Friction began in 1974 when LaVey disbanded the grotto system. Leadership within that system had been the basis of degrees. Now LaVey announced that degrees would be based on other criteria, one of which was financial donation to the CoS. A career military man, Aquino took pride in his degrees. (In 1976, his office

---

[127] Flowers, *Lords of the Left-Hand Path*, p. 218.   [128] Aquino, *Church of Satan*, p. 42.

featured an "ego wall" displaying forty-seven degrees and awards.)[129] He was particularly upset that LaVey awarded the rank of magister to Tony Fazzini, who acted as a chauffeur for the LaVeys. Aquino accused LaVey of simony. After a heated exchange of letters, Aquino tendered his resignation on June 10, 1975, writing to LaVey and Hegarty, "Since you – Satan's High Priest and High Priestess – have presumed to destroy these standards and replace the true Church of Satan with a 'Church of Anton,' the Infernal Mandate is hereby withdrawn from the organization known as the 'Church of Satan, Inc.'"[130] Using the mailing list for *The Cloven Hoof*, he urged other members to defect. Twenty-eight CoS members left with him.[131]

The break between Aquino and LaVey was not just about money or degrees: it was also about the supernatural. LaVey had long been ambiguous on this topic. Among his "Eleven Satanic Rules of the Earth," published in 1967, is, "Acknowledge the power of magic if you have employed it successfully to obtain your desires. If you deny the power of magic after having called upon it with success, you will lose all you have obtained."[132] But despite his frequent discussion of magic, LaVey also insisted that Satanism is a materialist philosophy. The way Aquino interpreted this paradox was that all discussion of Satan as symbolic was only the public, exoteric teaching of the CoS. As he put it:

> Satan is a symbol of the self, then, as it should be within the Satanist. But this symbolism is only part of the truth, because man's very ability to think and act in disregard of the "balancing factor" of the Universe necessitates a source for that ability. And that source is thus the intelligence that made the Church of Satan far more than an exercise in psychodramatic narcissism. It is the intelligence of what mankind has personified as the Prince of Darkness himself – no symbol or allegory, but a sentient being. This was the central "secret" – and the heart – of the Church of Satan.[133]

Sociologist Steven Foertsch suggests the issue *became* philosophical after the split.[134] It may be that Aquino's departure finally rendered untenable LaVey's effort to have it both ways on the supernatural. Today, the CoS defines itself unambiguously as endorsing "a materialist, atheist philosophy."[135]

According to Aquino, he performed a ritual on the night of the summer solstice, June 21, 1975, for the purpose of summoning Satan to ask where to lead those who defected from the CoS. Aquino experienced automatic writing and between midnight and four in the morning on June 22, he produced a text

---

[129] G. van Zack, "Local Satan Worshippers Get Set," *Daily Nexus* 57.44 (November 12, 1976): 1.
[130] Aquino, *Church of Satan*, pp. 833–4.
[131] Boulware, "A Devil of a Time"; Lyons, *Satan Wants You*, p. 126.
[132] LaVey, "Eleven Satanic Rules of the Earth."   [133] Aquino, *Church of Satan*, pp. 57–8.
[134] Foertsch, "Organizational Analysis," p. 68.   [135] Gilmore, "Yes, We Have No Occultism."

called "The Book of Coming Forth by Night."[136] The title references "The Book of Coming Forth by Day," a name for the Egyptian Book of the Dead. In this text, Satan declared, "Reconsecrate my Temple and my Order in the true name of Set. No longer will I accept the bastard title of a Hebrew fiend."[137] Aquino came to believe that Satan was actually Set, the Egyptian god of darkness, and that the Hebrew word *Satan* was derived from the Egyptian *Set-hen*, meaning "Majesty of Set."[138] With this revelation, Aquino set about professing a new religion, which he saw as continuation of the work started by the CoS.

For Setians, Set is the only true god. Set is unnatural in that he exists outside the natural universe and is therefore the only being capable of disrupting nature's mindless patterns. God, as conceived by most monotheistic religions, is equated in Aquino's philosophy with these static patterns. Individuality and consciousness are Promethean gifts Set bestowed to humans, which Setians call the Black Flame. Aquino even suggested that organic life is Set's doing as it is known to exist on only one planet and seems too unlikely to have occurred through random chance.[139]

For all this, Setians do not worship Set. Rather, they seek to become more like Set through a process called *xeper* (pronounced "coffer"), an Egyptian word meaning "to come into being." *Xeper* involves both study and ritual and, for many Setians, its ultimate goal is a form of immortality. Inspired by Plato, Aquino postulated the existence of both an objective universe and a transcendent, subjective universe. Ritual workings performed in the subjective universe may have consequences in the objective one. Setians create a magical double to operate within the subjective universe called a *ka*, an ancient Egyptian word meaning "soul." Toward this end, all Setians must adopt a magical name to use during rituals. Many choose the names of Egyptian deities.

LaVey dismissed the ToS as "a rip-off group," "New Age or Christian Satanism," and even "Laurel and Hardy's *Sons of the Desert*."[140] Some Setians and scholars have come to describe the ToS as "post-Satanism."[141] The ToS is certainly a left-hand path tradition and historically connected to Satanism, but the biblical character of Satan has been completely purged from its mythology.

---

[136] L. Kahaner, *Cults That Kill: Probing the Underworld of Occult Crime* (New York: Warner Books, 1988), p. 74.

[137] Quoted in Van Luijk, *Children of Lucifer*, p. 352.

[138] Flowers, *Lords of the Left-Hand Path*, p. 232.   [139] Ibid., p. 234.

[140] Aquino, *Church of Satan*, p. 420.

[141] K. Granholm, "The Left-Hand Path and Post-Satanism: The Temple of Set and the Evolution of Satanism," in P. Faxneld and J. A. Petersen (eds.), *The Devil's Party: Satanism in Modernity* (New York: Oxford University Press, 2013), pp. 209–28.

On October 23, 1975, Aquino registered the ToS as a nonprofit religious corporation, making this one of the first Satanic organizations to receive this status. He organized his group similarly to the CoS, but with more focus on ranks and discipline. Local chapters are known as pylons, a reference to gates of Egyptian temples. The administration is led by a high priest or priestess who is elected by a Council of Nine. There is also an executive director. The degree system is similar to that of the CoS but includes an additional rank of ipsissimus or ipsissima. Promotion to each rank involves working through an extensive reading list. New members are given one year to join a pylon and two years to reach the second degree of adept by showing proficiency in magic or their memberships are discontinued. Setians who are not part of the leadership normally never rise above this rank. Adepts have one year to join one of several suborganizations known as orders. There are numerous orders, each of which has a different focus. Examples include the Order of the Vampyre, the Order of Leviathan, and the Order of the Trapezoid. Setians also hold regular international meetings known as conclaves, something Aquino had organized for the CoS during the grotto era.

By the end of the 1970s, the ToS had an estimated 100 members with pylons in Detroit, Los Angeles, Washington, DC, New York, and San Jose, California.[142] Exact membership is unknown, but it is believed the ToS never had more than a few hundred members. In 1979, Aquino resigned as high priest and was replaced by Ronald Keith Barrett (1944–98). Barrett stepped down from this position in May 1982 and Aquino resumed his role as high priest. Barrett formed a schismatic organization called the Temple of Anubis, which continued until the early 2010s.[143]

In October 1982, Aquino traveled to the ruins of Castle Wewelsburg in Germany, where Heinrich Himmler (1900–45), leader of the Nazi SS, had performed neo-pagan rituals. Aquino had long been fascinated with Nazi occultism, although he claimed this did not indicate sympathy for their politics.[144] At the castle, Aquino performed a series of rituals and received a revelation from Set known as the Wewelsburg Working. The content of this revelation was an insight into the difficult nature of running an organized satanic religion: celebrating individuality and self-determination is incompatible with a structured organization.

Outsiders were less concerned with the content of the Wewelsburg Working than with Aquino's apparent connection to Nazism. Defectors from the ToS leaked writings about the Wewelsburg Working, including William Butch, who

---

[142] Lyons, *Satan Wants You*, p. 130.   [143] Introvigne, *Satanism*, p. 351.

[144] J. Adler and P. Abramson, "The Second Beast of Revelation," *Newsweek* (November 16, 1987): p. 73.

founded a short-lived group called the Temple of Nepthys, and Linda Blood, whose book *The New Satanists* (1994) became a significant text in the Satanic Panic. The constellation of a military intelligence officer, Satanism, and Nazism proved irresistible to conspiracy theorists. Soon conspiracy theorists such as David Icke and William Cooper were citing the Wewelsburg Working as evidence of a vast Satanist–Nazi conspiracy.

In 1986, Aquino became embroiled in a child molestation case at the Presidio army base in San Francisco, where he worked. Gary Hambright (1953–90), a Baptist pastor who worked at a daycare facility at the base, was charged with child molestation. When the children were interviewed, they identified Aquino and his wife, Lilith, among their abusers. In August 1987, police raided the Aquinos' residence, but no charges were ever brought against the Aquinos, who were able to prove that they had been in Washington, DC, when the alleged abuse occurred. It is possible the children were coached into identifying the Aquinos or had previously seen them on talk shows. However, the accusation continued to be a talking point for conspiracy theorists, who claimed the military was protecting Aquino.

In 1996, Don Webb became high priest. In 2002, he was succeeded by Zeena Schreck, who resigned after only six weeks. Aquino resumed his position as high priest until 2004 when he was replaced by Patricia Hardy. Aquino died in July 2020 at the age of seventy-three.

Amoral Groups and the Order of Nine Angles

A few Satanists truly revere Satan as a god of evil rather than a Promethean figure and regard groups like CoS and ToS as too benevolent and law-abiding to be called Satanists. During the 1990s, this attitude became particularly common in the extreme metal music scene, where there was social pressure to distinguish oneself as more extreme – and therefore more authentic – than other musicians or fans. Norwegian metal producer Øystein Aarseth, also known as Euronymous, declared, "I believe in [a] horned devil, a personified Satan. In my opinion, all other forms of Satanism are bullshit."[145] Aarseth managed a black metal band called Mayhem. He and his colleagues embraced Satanism, Stalinism, Nazism, and racist forms of Norse heathenism. Massimo Introvigne opined on their brand of reactive Satanism: "They mixed Satanism, paganism, and radical politics in a sort of primitive cocktail. It was not culturally sophisticated, but it was dangerous."[146] In 1992, Kristian "Varg" Vikernes became the new bassist for Mayhem. Aarseth and Vikernes began a series of

---

[145] Quoted in Introvigne, *Satanism*, p. 479.   [146] Ibid., p. 482.

arson attacks on Norway's historic stave churches. Vikernes murdered Aarseth in 1993 after the pair had a falling out.

Another group, the Misanthropic Luciferian Order (MLO), which was founded in Sweden in 1995 and later renamed the Temple of Black Light, was also comprised primarily of metal musicians. The group's foundational texts, the *Liber Azerate* and *Liber Falxifer*, describe a cosmology that combines Satanism with Gnosticism and Kabbalah. The group is "anti-cosmic" regarding the universe and see everything in it as a prison. Their stated goal is to undo creation and restore the universe to a state of primal chaos. The MLO members endorsed violence and their rituals included the sacrifice of cats. The group gained attention in 1997 when member Jon Nödtveidt (1975–2006) of the band Dissection, along with MLO leader Nemesis Shahin Khashnood-Sharis, aka Vlad (b. 1977), murdered a randomly selected gay man, Algerian immigrant Josef Ben Meddour (1960–97). Both served several years in prison. In 2006, Nödtveidt committed suicide. It was reported that next to his body were found candles and a satanic book, likely *Liber Azerate*.[147]

The so-called sinister tradition is a milieu of antinomian and amoral Satanic (or post-Satanic) groups. These groups typically have only a handful of members but often exert a disproportionate influence on the satanic milieu by disseminating their writings online. Like the MLO, these groups advocate worldviews that have led to extremism. Religion scholar Jacob Senholt lists seven characteristics typical of the sinister tradition: 1) "anti-ethics" or rejection of morality; 2) right-wing politics, including endorsement of Nazism, racism, and social Darwinism; 3) an emphasis on physical training, including survival skills as part of initiation; 4) support of direct action, including infiltrating government organizations, assassination, and terrorism; 5) specialized vocabulary associated with this tradition; 6) promotion of traditional Satanism, including belief in supernatural forces; and 7) rejection of any "Semitic" influences, including Christian elements or esoteric traditions such as Kabbalah, often in favor of elements from European paganism.[148]

The ur-type that defines the sinister tradition is the Order of the Nine Angles (ONA), which formed in the United Kingdom around the 1970s. Writers in the ONA sometimes describe their practice as traditional Satanism in contrast to the ideas of LaVey or Aquino. In 1994, an ONA member using the pseudonym Christos Beest told an interviewer:

---

[147] Ibid., p. 509.
[148] J. C. Senholt, "The Sinister Tradition: Political Esotericism and the Convergence of Radical Islam, Satanism, and National Socialism in the Order of Nine Angles" (Master's Thesis, University of Amsterdam, 2009), pp. 12–13.

> A lot of people at the Temple of Set and the Church of Satan are trying to reestablish Satanism as a moral religion. Something which is sanitized, something which is misunderstood and really quite nice. What the ONA is doing is countering that by saying, "No, it isn't." It's regaining the original darkness of what Satanism is, because if Satanism isn't evil, what is?[149]

The ONA has earned its sinister reputation through affiliation with neo-Nazis and other extremist groups. The ONA writings also insist that human sacrifice, or culling, is the sin qua non of Satanism.

The ONA literature claims the group is part of a thousand-year-old tradition from Albion (an ancient name for England) that worships dark gods. According to this history, the ONA was formed when an anonymous Grand Mistress united three pagan groups called Camlad, the Temple of the Sun, and the Noctulians in the late 1960s. The Grand Mistress initiated Anton Long – a pseudonym used by the author of most ONA material – in 1973. She then left for Australia, leaving Long to succeed her as Grand Master.

If this story is true, it would mean the ONA began around the same time as LaVey's CoS. However, Long's writings can be dated back only to 1976, by which time the CoS and ToS were already established.[150] This has led to speculation about whether the ONA was actually inspired by these predecessors. Luijk notes that the ONA's advocacy for brutality and affinity for neo-Nazism can be read as "an extreme extrapolation of tendencies already present in LaVeyan Satanism."[151] Additionally, Aquino composed a ritual called the Ceremony of Nine Angles that appeared in LaVey's book *The Satanic Rituals* in 1972. The ONA claims this connection is a coincidence and their nine angles refer to the sevenfold Tree of Wyrd associated with the seven planets, plus system as a whole, and "the mystery of the abyss."[152]

Most scholars assume the ONA was founded by David Myatt, who writes as Anton Long, although it is possible multiple people have written as Long. Myatt has denied being Long; however, Senholt discovered copies of ONA documents from 1978 with Myatt's name on them and early ONA texts were published

---

[149] Baddeley, *Lucifer Rising*, p. 164.

[150] N. Goodrick-Clarke, *Black Sun: Aryan Cults Esoteric Nazism and the Politics of Identity* (New York: New York University Press, 2002), p. 21.

[151] Van Luijk, *Children of Lucifer*, p. 371.

[152] Senholt, "The Sinister Tradition," p. 27. Curiously, Graham Harvey, writing in 1995, gives an entirely different account of the symbolism of the nine angles: "In brief, the Universe is said to be divided between the ordinary or 'causal realm' and the 'acausal realm.' The dimensions of these realms intersect at nine angles: three of space, one of 'causal' (or linear) time, two symbolically seen as 'positive' and 'negative' (though in essence these are one) and one of acausal 'time'" ("Satanism in Britain Today," *Journal of Contemporary Religion* 10.3 [1995], 292–3). It seems likely that the symbolism of the nine angles has changed over time.

through a press Myatt owned.[153] Myatt was born around 1950 to a British family working in Tanzania. He moved to England in the 1960s, where he joined a prominent neo-Nazi organization and became a bodyguard for one of its leaders. In the 1990s, Myatt was involved in the National Socialist Movement (NSM), a British neo-Nazi group, and wrote tracts on "Aryan Revolution." In 1999, another NSM member, David Copeland, was arrested for a series of bomb attacks that killed three and injured 129. It was speculated that Copeland was inspired by one of Myatt's texts that contains recommendations for assassination and terror bombings.[154] During this period, the ONA released a newsletter called "Temple 88" ("H is the eighth letter of the alphabet and 88 is neo-Nazi code for "Heil Hitler"). Additionally, some ONA texts use a dating system that measures time from 1889 – the year of Hitler's birth. Thus 2023 CE would be 134 "Yf" or "Year of the Führer."[155]

In 1998, Myatt announced his conversion to Islam. He began studying Arabic and attending Friday services at a mosque. However, he maintained connections with the NSM and ONA. During this period, Myatt called for violent jihad against the West and wrote an essay defending suicide attacks as consistent with Islamic law. In 2010, Myatt announced that he now rejected Islam in favor of his personal philosophy that he called the Numinous Way or "pathei-mathos" (learning through adversity). Myatt claims he now rejects intolerance and extremism in favor of compassion for others. As discussed in what follows, there is ample reason to doubt whether any of Myatt's conversions were sincere or if they were part of a sinister game.

"Anton Long" and a few others have written voluminous amounts of metaphysical theory, manifestos, and novels. Senholt estimates that the ONA has produced more literature than the CoS and TOS combined.[156] Part of the ONA's appeal seems to be the detailed worldview and specific vocabulary described in this literature, which often resembles that of a successful science fiction series. Like Aquino's objective and subjective universes, the ONA postulates a material, causal world and a supernatural, acausal world. The acausal world is home to the dark gods, including Baphomet (imagined as female in ONA literature) and Atazoth, a deity inspired by horror writer Howard P. Lovecraft. The act of bringing acausal energies and beings into the casual world through magic is called presencing. Nexions are liminal spaces between the two worlds. This term can refer to special places or people and it has come to refer to local ONA groups.

Human sacrifice may be performed by magically cursing the victim, arranging an accident, or literal murder. Victims are called *opfers* – a German word for

---

[153] Senholt, "The Sinister Tradition," pp. 47–8.   [154] Ibid., p. 42.   [155] Ibid., p. 7.
[156] Ibid., p. 36.

"sacrifice" and also the name of a rune invented by the Nazi SS.[157] The ONA literature describes selecting *opfers* carefully and covertly testing them. Those deemed cowardly or otherwise unworthy are to be culled. Writing in 2001, Lewis expressed his suspicion that the ONA's rhetoric about culling was "macho posturing" and a way to draw attention to the group.[158] But more recently contemporary terror networks appear to be putting this ideology into practice.

The ONA espouses a theory of history in which time is divided into aeons, each associated with a particular civilization. The ONA believes it is possible to manipulate the energies of these aeons through aeonic magic, thereby preserving a civilization, causing one to crumble, or calling a new one into being. The present aeon is considered corrupted as Western civilization has fallen under the influence of the Magian system or simply the System. *Magians* is a term used in neo-Nazi subculture to indicate Jews and Christians. (Neo-Nazi Francis Parker Jockey [1917–60] called Jews Magians in the belief that modern Jews actually practice a form of Zoroastrianism.)[159]

The ONA's tactics can be described as accelerationist in that they hope to use violence to spur a larger conflict resulting in the collapse of Western civilization. They advocate infiltrating other extreme political and esoteric groups in pursuit of this goal. Their literature endorses murder and other crimes because this is thought to weaken the System. The ONA's millennial goal involves creating a race of sinister god-men through intense self-initiation and training that will one day colonize space. Myatt wrote, "The ultimate Destiny of the Aryan race lies in the conquest of Outer Space – in the creation of a Galactic Empire."[160] The ONA literature also predicts a messiah figure called Vindex (Latin for avenger) who will have unprecedented control of acausal (magical) forces and usher in the collapse of the Magian system. In a possible softening of Myatt's Aryan ideology, ONA writings state that Vindex may be of either gender and any ethnicity.

Like the CoS and ToS, the ONA has a system of grades. However, there is no central authority and the order's seven grades are designed to be achieved entirely through a series of self-initiations called the Seven-Fold Way or Hebdomadry.[161] Advancing requires mastering survival skills as well as mental and emotional challenges. One initiation involves lying on the ground all night

---

[157] D. Miller, "Beyond The Iron Gates: How Nazi-Satanists Infiltrated the UK Underground, *The Quietus* (November 27, 2018). https://goo.by/rkhegR.

[158] J. R. Lewis, *Satanism Today: An Encyclopedia of Religion, Folklore, and Popular Culture* (Santa Barbara, CA: ABC–CLIO, 2002), p. 196.

[159] Introvigne, *Satanism*, pp. 360–1. [160] Quoted in Senholt, "The Sinister Tradition," p. 48.

[161] C. R. Monette, *Mysticism in the 21st Century* (Wilsonville, OR: Sirius Academic Press, 2013), pp. 86–7.

and contemplating the stars without falling asleep. Another requires the initiate to live in total isolation in the wilderness, without modern equipment, for three months. Yet another requires the initiate to form their own esoteric group – which may be one reason there are so many ephemeral groups associated with ONA.

Initiates must also complete what they call insight roles. This is somewhat like an internship in which the initiate joins a group or takes on a career that is at odds with their normal system of values. An initiate who has issues with authority may join the police or the military as part of an insight role. Significantly, joining neo-Nazi groups and Islamic terror cells are listed as examples of insight roles in the ONA literature. Therefore, when figures such as Myatt claim to have converted to Islam or to have renounced extremism, it is impossible to tell whether these conversions are actually insight role training, infiltration, or sincere. Likewise, it is difficult to judge whether ONA groups are infiltrating extremist groups or whether these groups are using the ONA to radicalize esotericists.

The ONA often resembles an internet meme more than an actual group. In 1995, religion scholar Graham Harvey wrote, "I suggest that the ONA consists of less than 10 people and perhaps fewer than five."[162] Occultists sometimes jokingly called it the order of no members. But in recent decades, a larger audience has encountered ONA material online, where it has proven popular with white supremacist groups and troubled young men. There are now several far-right groups connected to the ONA, including the Tempel ov Blood (original spelling) based in South Carolina, the White Star Acception in California, the Black Order in New Zealand, and the Temple of THEM in Australia. Each of these groups has continued to evolve, creating new traditions and vocabulary. By one 2013 estimate, as many as 2,000 people may be associated with the ONA in one form or another.[163] Although most ONA affiliates are solitary or organized into small cells, they describe themselves as sharing a common tradition or being sinister tribes. Some sign their electronic communications ISS for "in sinister solidarity."[164]

The ONA materials were spread through a neo-Nazi web forum called Iron March that existed between 2011 and 2017. The terrorist network Atomwaffen Division formed on this site in 2015. It now promotes ONA ideas on less public sectors of the Internet. In 2018, Atomwaffen member Sam Woodward murdered nineteen-year-old Blaze Bernstein, who was gay and Jewish. The Combating

---

[162] Harvey, "Satanism in Britain Today," p. 292.

[163] Monette, *Mysticism in the 21st Century*, p. 89.

[164] George Sieg, "Angular Momentum: From Traditional to Progressive Satanism in the Order of Nine Angles," *International Journal for the Study of New Religions* 4.2 (2013): pp. 251–82.

Terrorism Center at West Point speculated that Bernstein's murder had been a culling consistent with the ONA literature.[165]

In June 2020, nineteen-year-old Danyal Hussein murdered Bibaa Henry and Nicole Smallman in a park in London. Police found a pact Hussein had signed with his own blood in which he promised to murder women for a demon named Lucifuge Rofocale in exchange for winning the Mega Millions Super Jackpot. Hussein appears to have gotten this idea from Matthew Lawrence, better known as E. A. Koetting, an internet personality and self-described black magician from Utah. Koetting wrote that he had joined "an American cell of the notorious British Order of Nine Angles."[166] This was likely a reference to the Tempel ov Blood, whose books Koetting promoted in his YouTube videos.

That same month, a twenty-two-year-old American soldier named Ethan Melzer sent his unit's location, movements, and security plans to an ONA cell via the encrypted Telegram messaging system. According to the FBI, which intercepted these communications, this information was to be passed on to jihadists who would use it to ambush Melzer's unit. Melzer had apparently been a Satanist for some time before joining the military and the betrayal of his unit was consistent with ONA ideas of culling.[167] Melzer's attorney pled that ONA was a "ridiculous cult" and that joining it was a sign of his client's immaturity because it was obviously "absurd, dangerous and not worth following." But District Judge Gregory Woods ordered the maximum sentence of forty-five years in prison, adding, "His crimes were committed to destroy civilization."[168]

In 2021, it was revealed that Tempel ov Blood founder, Joshua Caleb Sutter of South Carolina, had been working as an FBI informant since 2003 and had been paid more than $140,000 for his help.[169] During this time, Sutter published a variety of ONA texts through his Martinet Press, including *Iron Gates* (2014), a novel about a post-apocalyptic world ruled by fascist Satanic cults that engage in pedophilia and human sacrifice. "Iron Gates now!" has reportedly become a slogan used by Atomwaffen.

---

[165] H. E. Upchurch, "The Iron March Forum and the Evolution of the "Skull Mask" Neo-Fascist Network," *Combating Terrorism Center Sentinel* 14.10 (December 2021). https://goo.by/Hznwdj.

[166] Emily Pennink, "Social Media Giants under Pressure over Satanist Linked to Wembley Murders," *Evening Standard* (October 20, 2021). https://goo.by/eNrYza.

[167] Ali Winston, "Neo-Nazi Satanist Cult Is a Terrorist Group, Feds Say," *Rolling Stone* (July 6, 2022). https://goo.by/sXRlWe.

[168] Josh Russell, "Army Soldier Who Plotted Unit Ambush with Satanic Neo-Nazi Cult Sentenced to 45 Years," *Courthouse News Service* (March 3, 2013). https://goo.by/UczIsL.

[169] Matthew Gault, "FBI Bankrolled Publisher of Occult Neo-Nazi Books, Feds Claim," Vice.com (August 25, 2021). https://bit.ly/3tUtLdf.

Other Esoteric Groups

Joy of Satan was founded in 2002 by Maxine Dietrich. Its mythology combines Satanism, the so-called ancient aliens hypothesis, and antisemitic ideology. Borrowing from the theories of Zecharia Sitchin (1920–2010), Joy of Satan literature claims the Nordic-Aryan race was genetically engineered by benevolent aliens known as Enki or Satan, while an evil alien race called Reptilians created Jews. After the Enki left 10,000 years ago, the Jews created false religions, including Christianity, slandered the benevolent aliens as devils, and stigmatized sexuality. The Joy of Satan advocates communing with the devils/aliens through meditation and certain forms of sexual magic.

In 2006, it was revealed that Maxine Dietrich's real name was Andrea Herrington – her pseudonym was an apparent reference to German singer and actress Marlene Dietrich (1901–92), who was popular among Nazi Party officials. Moreover, Andrea's husband was Cliff Herrington, who cofounded the NSM, one of the largest neo-Nazi groups in the United States. This discovery caused turmoil for both groups as many NSM members did not wish to be associated with Satanism and many Satanists did not wish to be associated with the NSM. Herrington was forced out of the NSM and several tiny groups splintered off Joy of Satan, including the House of Enlightenment, Enki's Black Temple, the Siaion, the Knowledge of Satan Group, and the temple of the Ancients.[170]

The Satanic Reds, founded by Tani Jantsang in 1997, was an esoteric Satanic group whose logo was a communist hammer and sickle over a pentagram with the words "Power to the People – Join the Revolution." Despite this symbolism, Jantsang's political essays praise Franklin Delano Roosevelt and seem to promote New Deal progressivism more than communism. Jantsang became interested in esotericism in the 1960s and came to believe that Lovecraft had knowledge of secret dark doctrines that had roots in central Asia. She herself claimed Mongolian descent and began producing material about this "dark tradition" in 1989. For a time, she maintained correspondence with the CoS, especially Barton, before forming her own organization. Jantsang's writing claimed these dark doctrines linked Satanism to Indian Tantra, Turanian mysticism, and the teachings of Pythagoras. Much as Aquino reinterpreted the etymology of the name Satan, Jantsang claimed it is derived from the Sanskrit words "Sat" and "Tan," meaning "being" and "becoming." Ancient Israelites feared these cosmic forces, causing them to interpret Satan as evil.

Online discussion about theistic Satanism suggests there are many theistic Satanists who are solitary practitioners and have no formal affiliation with any

---

[170] Introvigne, *Satanism*, pp. 370–1.

of the groups discussed here. Diane Vera has been active for years in providing online resources for theistic Satanists. Her own group, the Church of Azazel, has organized gatherings and rituals for Satanists in New York.[171]

6 Satanic Panic

Just before Halloween 1988, a kitten was found in a locker in Aurora Hills Middle School in Aurora, Colorado. The kitten was unharmed, but someone had given the poor creature a mohawk haircut and adorned it with pentagram earrings. In response, police sergeant Monte Landers called a meeting about the dangers of Satanism. He told 200 assembled parents, "It's in our government. It's in our schools. . . . The person sitting next to you in church may be a Satanist."[172] Similar incidents were occurring throughout North America, the United Kingdom, and Australia in a pattern now remembered as the Satanic Panic.

The Satanic Panic was a conspiracy theory that claimed a network of criminal Satanists murdered thousands of people a year. A psychiatrist who endorsed such claims in a psychiatric journal called it "a hidden holocaust."[173] The Satanists allegedly got away with these crimes because they had infiltrated the media and law enforcement. No bodies were ever found because morticians and crematorium operators were also part of the conspiracy. Or, in some versions, the Satanists used certain women as breeders, giving birth to numerous babies just so Satanists could sacrifice them without anyone noticing a missing person. Soon a class of moral entrepreneurs emerged, claiming to be either experts in Satanic crime or ex-Satanists who had converted to Christianity.

At the 1980 annual meeting of the American Psychiatric Association in New Orleans, Louisiana, Lawrence Pazder coined the term "ritual abuse," adding a new element to the conspiracy theory.[174] Pazder had spent hundreds of hours with his patient – and eventual wife – Michelle Proby, doing hypnotic regression to uncover Proby's repressed memories. The narrative constructed through this process was published in 1980 as *Michelle Remembers*. It described how Michelle's mother tortured her for days in elaborate satanic rituals when she was only five. At the climax of this torture, a portal to hell opened and Satan himself appeared, only to be defeated by the Virgin Mary and the archangel Michael (Mary removed all of Michelle's scars, eliminating any physical evidence of the torture).

[171] Ibid., p. 527.
[172] Quoted in A. Hernandez, "Satanic Panic in Colorado," Denverlibrary.org (December 7, 2021). https://history.denverlibrary.org/news/satanic-panic.
[173] R. P. Kluft, "Reflections on Allegations of Ritual Abuse," *Dissociation* 3.4 (December 1989), pp. 191–3 (p. 192).
[174] Kahaner, *Cults That Kill*, pp. 200–1.

Michelle Remembers was immediately debunked. In addition to testimony from Michelle's father and two sisters, the St. Margaret's School yearbook for 1955/6 features a class photo taken in November 1955 in which Proby can be seen attending school and appears healthy. (According to Pazder's book, Michelle spent that November imprisoned in a basement.)[175] But the book was still a bestseller. More importantly, it introduced the concept of SRA, in which children were allegedly so traumatized they could not remember the abuse. This belief necessitated a new class of therapists who could induce adults to remember their experiences of satanic ritual abuse.

Police and social workers were trained to look for signs of SRA. At a statewide conference held in New Hampshire in May 1989, police claimed there were 2 million Satanists in the United States, organized into "criminal cartels."[176] At the height of the panic, legislatures in several states began proposing laws banning devil worship. Such laws would have been a serious blow to religious freedom as guaranteed in the Constitution.[177]

Of course, there were groups of organized Satanists active in the 1980s. There were also lone criminals such as Richard Ramirez who identified as Satanists. What does not seem to have existed was a satanic group that was both criminal and organized. Certainly no such group was capable of murdering thousands of people or infiltrating the government. LaVey said of such conspiracies, "It's too bad stupidity isn't painful. Then maybe some of these people would go get some help."[178]

Origins of the Satanic Panic

While bizarre, the claims of the Satanic Panic were not unprecedented. In earlier times, Jews and witches were accused of blending in with the population while secretly performing horrible rituals and harming innocent children. Before that, early Christians were suspected of murdering babies and holding incestuous orgies. As discussed in Section 1, such claims function to explain misfortune and reinforce the existing social order.[179] But this insight alone does not explain why this particular panic surfaced in the 1980s or why it took the shape that it did.

One significant influence on the panic was horror films, particularly the so-called unholy trinity of films that emerged near the beginning of the panic: *Rosemary's Baby* (1968), *The Exorcist* (1973), and *The Omen* (1976). *Rosemary's Baby* was especially influential because it portrayed Satanists as

---

[175] D. Nathan and M. R. Snedeker, *Satan's Silence: Ritual Abuse and the Making of a Modern American Witch Hunt* (New York: Basic Books 1995), p. 24.

[176] Ibid., p. 76.

[177] J. Victor, "Satanic Cult Rumors As Contemporary Legend," *Western Folklore* 49.1 (1990), 51–81 (p. 76).

[178] Lyons, *Satan Wants You*, p. 138.   [179] Frankfurter, *Evil Incarnate*.

friendly and normal-looking neighbors and professionals.[180] When therapists hypnotized patients to recover memories of SRA, many seemed to be recalling scenes from these films. For example, in *Michelle Remembers*, the Satanists bring in a possessed woman. Regressed to age five, Michelle recalls, "She drools a lot and her head starts to go all funny and spins around."[181] This scene is highly derivative of *The Exorcist*.

Another important influence was the so-called cult wars of the 1970s.[182] There was a surge of new religious movements (NRMs) in the 1960s due to the immigration reform that allowed missionaries for Asian religions, as well as the counterculture of the baby boomer generation. The CoS, formed in 1966, was part of this historical moment. Moral entrepreneurs claimed that cults used brainwashing or similar forms of mental manipulation to forcibly convert innocents. The fear of NRMs died down, but fear of brainwashing rituals shifted to satanic conspiracies. During the cult wars, families could hire deprogrammers to abduct family members who had converted to NRMs and sequester them in an attempt to reverse cult brainwashing. In 1973, Ted Patrick, the so-called father of deprogramming, was hired to abduct two adult women who had left home and moved in together. According to the women's strict Greek Orthodox parents, their independence indicated involvement with Satanism and required deprogramming.[183]

In particular, the 1969 murders orchestrated by Charles Manson convinced many that the spiritual movements of the counterculture were dangerous and manipulative. Among the victims of the Manson Family was Sharon Tate, the wife of Roman Polanski, who directed *Rosemary's Baby*. Polanski told Lieutenant Earl Deemer of the Los Angeles Police, "It could be some kind of witchcraft, you know."[184] In 1970, the far-right John Birch Society published an article titled "Satanism: A Practical Guide to Witch Hunting" that declared Satanism "the fastest growing criminal menace of our time," second only to communism. The article connected Manson, Polanski, and LaVey, incorrectly asserting that LaVey was "an ardent socialist" and that he consulted on *Rosemary's Baby*.[185]

In 1972, Mike Warnke published his memoir *The Satan Seller*, which became one of the most important early texts of the panic. Warnke claimed to have led

---

[180]   D. Frankfurter, "Awakening to Satanic Conspiracy: *Rosemary's Baby* and the Cult Next Door," in M. D. Eckel and B. L. Herling (eds.), *Deliver Us from Evil: Boston University Studies in Philosophy and Religion* (New York: Continuum, 2011), pp. 75–86.

[181]   M. Smith and L. Pazder, *Michelle Remembers* (New York: Pocket Books, 1980), p. 159.

[182]   D. G. Bromley, "Satanism: The New Cult Scare" in J. T. Richardson, J. Best, and D. G. Bromley (eds.), *The Satanism Scare* (Hawthorne, NY: Aldine De Gruyter, 1991), pp. 49–74 (p. 49).

[183]   Hernandez, "Satanic Panic in Colorado."   [184]   Schreck, *Satanic Screen*, p. 139.

[185]   D. E. Gumaer, "Satanism: A Practical Guide to Witch-Hunting," *American Opinion* 13.8 (September 1970), 41–8.

a group of 1,500 Satanists that engaged in rape and human sacrifice before he converted to evangelical Christianity. Dominican theology professor Richard Woods, however, described *The Satan Seller* as "a paranoid fantasy of Christian fascism."[186] But it became a bestseller, winning accolades in *Moody Monthly* and *The Christian Century.* Warnke began touring America in a trailer called the Witchmobile. In 1991, the evangelical magazine *Cornerstone* thoroughly debunked *The Satan Seller,* but the damage had been done.

Rumors sometimes resulted in police action, as happened in an event known as the Toledo Dig. Shortly after *20/20* aired a report on Satanism, Sheriff James Telb of Lucas County, Ohio, announced that several confidential informants had alerted him to a satanic cult. The cult was said to have been active since 1969 and had as many as 200 members. It was also said to have sacrificed up to fifty people, most of them children.[187] On June 21 and 22, 1985, fifty law enforcement officers from multiple states gathered to excavate a wooded lot, looking for evidence of the cult, while more than 100 reporters watched. Bits of trash were uncovered and declared to be occult ritual relics, but no Satanists were apprehended, nor were any bodies found.

Satanic Ritual Abuse

While police fruitlessly searched for the bodies of sacrifice victims, SRA conspiracy theories now claimed the victims of the Satanists were hiding in plain sight: they were either small children who were incapable of talking about their abuse or adults like Michelle Proby who had repressed memories of childhood abuse. The assumptions underlying SRA theories go back to the early work of Sigmund Freud. In 1896, Freud presented a new theory that hysteria is caused by repressed memories of trauma, usually childhood sexual abuse and if the therapist can dredge up these memories, the hysteria resolves itself. But there were problems with this theory, and Freud began to question whether all hysteria was caused by early sexual trauma. When he urged patients to recall their childhood trauma, some began to describe such details as cannibalism and satanic rituals. He began to suspect that these were not memories but fantasies – perhaps even fantasies he had encouraged. By October 1887, he had abandoned this theory of hysteria.[188]

Several factors led to the revival of Freud's theory in the twentieth century. The 1957 film *The Three Faces of Eve,* based on a psychiatric report of a woman diagnosed with multiple personality disorder (MPD), inspired popular interest

---

[186] R. Woods, *The Devil* (Chicago, IL: Thomas More Press, 1974), p. 43.

[187] J. Norris and J. A. Potter, "The Devil Made Me Do It," *Penthouse* (January 1986), 50.

[188] Introvigne, *Satanism*, p. 377.

in this diagnosis – today known as dissociative identity disorder. The 1976 film *Sybil* also popularized MPD and was based on the work of psychiatrist Cornelia B. Wilbur (1908–92) and her patient Shirley Ardell Mason (1923–98), whom Wilbur diagnosed as having multiple personalities resulting from severe childhood abuse. (Several researchers have suggested that Mason did not actually have multiple personalities and was encouraged by Wilbur to perform symptoms of MPD.)[189]

Wilbur popularized the idea that Freud had been right the first time. In this, she was joined by feminists such as social worker Florence Rush, who claimed Freud refused to believe his patients' stories of abuse. By the end of the 1970s, the elements of repressed memories, childhood trauma, and Satanism were all aligned and the stage was set for *Michelle Remembers*, which gave rise to widespread rumors of SRA. Pazder defined ritual abuse as "repeated physical, emotional, mental and spiritual assaults combined with a systematic use of symbols, ceremonies, and machinations designed and orchestrated to attain malevolent effects."[190] According to figures like Pazder, abusive rituals were actually a kind of psychological technology used by Satanists to effect ego destruction in children and thereby convert them to Satanism. Much as *Three Faces of Eve* and *Sybil* had caused people to suspect they had MPD, *Michelle Remembers* sent numerous people to therapists, suspecting that they too were repressing memories of SRA.

Psychiatrists began endorsing claims of SRA, particularly as they related to MPD. In 1980, "dissociation" was added to *The Diagnostic and Statistical Manual,* with MPD placed as the first disorder under this heading. New journals, organizations, and conferences were held to discuss MPD and these became vectors through which claims of SRA were spread. Psychologist Richard Noll points out that, ironically, this turn happened in part because psychiatry moved *away* from Freudian psychoanalysis toward a more biological model of treating mental illness with medication. A generation of psychiatrists who had been trained in psychoanalysis suddenly felt obsolete. But since MPD and other dissociative disorders were believed to be rooted in trauma, psychiatrists who diagnosed their patients with these disorders were again free to use a Freudian approach, sifting through their childhood memories instead of prescribing medication. In 1990, Noll was invited to speak on a conference panel on alternative explanations of SRA claims, and he questioned the existence of satanic cults. Afterward, several licensed mental health

---

[189] D. Nathan, *Sybil Exposed: The Extraordinary Story behind the Famous Multiple Personality Case* (New York Free Press 2011); R. Beck. *We Believe the Children: A Moral Panic in the 1980s* (New York: PublicAffairs, 2015).

[190] Kahaner, *Cults That Kill,* pp. 200–1.

professionals approached him and accused him of being a Satanist engaged in a disinformation campaign.[191]

Multiple personality disorder – often connected to claims of repressed memories – was overdiagnosed throughout the 1980s and by the 1990s, scores of people were suing therapists over treatment they underwent for MPD. The case of Patricia Burgus is but one example. Burgus was incorrectly diagnosed with MPD and from 1986 to 1992 she was hospitalized under the care of psychiatrist Bennet Braun, a key figure in claims of MPD and SRA. Braun treated Burgess with dangerous amounts of drugs and daily hypnosis sessions. Burgus came to believe that she had 300 personalities and that her parents were part of a satanic and cannibalistic cult. Braun even obtained a meatloaf prepared by Burgus's mother and had it tested for human proteins. When it came back negative, Braun continued to insist that Burgus's family were likely cannibals. Burgus came to believe that she herself was high priestess of a satanic cult and had cannibalized 2,000 children a year while her husband was at work. She also believed that she had abused her own children and her two sons – ages four and five – were also hospitalized and treated for cult abuse. Guilt over this belief drove Burgus to attempt suicide. Burgus's insurance company paid out more than $3 million for the family's treatment.[192]

After Burgus was transferred out of a special hospital unit Braun had created for dissociative disorders, the drugs began to wear off. She soon realized there had been no satanic cult and that Braun had planted these memories during hypnosis sessions. In addition, the dissociation unit housed multiple patients who had shared satanic delusions with each other, some of which were derived from *Michelle Remembers*. In fact, both Braun and FBI agent Kenneth Lanning, who debunked claims of organized criminal Satanists, agreed that they could find no reports of SRA that predated the publication of *Michelle Remembers*.[193] Pat Burgus sued Braun for malpractice as did several of his other patients. He finally surrendered his license to practice medicine in 2020.[194]

The McMartin Preschool Trial

The McMartin Preschool Trial (1984–90) became the most famous case of the Satanic Panic. It began when a single mother named Judy Johnson of Manhattan Beach, California, noticed her three-year-old son was experiencing discomfort

---

[191] R. Noll, "Speak, Memory," *Psychiatric Times* (March 19, 2014). psychiatrictimes.com/view/speak-memory.

[192] C. Hanson, "Dangerous Therapy: The Story of Patricia Burgus and Multiple Personality Disorder," *Chicago* (June 1, 1998). https://bit.ly/3sr1U3Q.

[193] R. Hicks, *In Pursuit of Satan: The Police and the Occult* (Buffalo, NY: Prometheus Books, 1991), pp. 176–7.

[194] State of Montana Board of Medical Examiners, "Final Order in the Matter of Bennett Braun: Case No. 2019-MED-95," (January 22, 2021).

around his anus. She came to believe her son had been sodomized at McMartin Preschool. She accused Raymond Buckey, the only male employee at the prestigious family-owned daycare center. Police took Johnson's claim seriously and sent a form letter to roughly 200 parents who had sent children to McMartin, asking them to question their children about sodomy, pornography, and similar topics.[195] Parents were alarmed and began to interpret ordinary childhood curiosity about sexuality as evidence of abuse. As more accusations came in, law enforcement concluded that this could not be the work of one individual and that the entire McMartin family must be involved in abusing children on a massive scale. Children were brought to a specialized abuse therapy clinic. Assuming the children were too traumatized to discuss their experiences openly, therapists employed dolls and puppets while urging them to reveal "yucky secrets." Many children seemed to have understood their statements as play and not testimony in a criminal case. They described tunnels beneath the school, being taken to other locations in planes or hot air balloons, and rituals involving lions and elephants. Children who denied abuse occurred were diagnosed as being in denial.[196] Based on this testimony, eight employees of McMartin Preschool were charged with 321 counts of child abuse involving forty-eight children.

One of the first people to introduce claims of SRA was Robert Currie, a retired television producer whose three sons had attended McMartin. Currie interviewed several children himself and advised Kenneth Wooden, who produced the *20/20* special "The Devil Worshippers."[197] Pazder was brought in to counsel children and aid the prosecution in their investigation. Soon many assumed the McMartin family were Satanists. The prosecution persisted with the case for years, even though no forensic evidence could be found and the original accuser, Judy Johnson, was hospitalized with acute schizophrenia. Prosecuting the case cost the public more than $15 million, making it the most expensive case in American history at the time.[198]

All charges were eventually dropped, although Buckey was imprisoned for five years during the trial. The McMartins' livelihood and reputations were destroyed and a vigilante set fire to their preschool.[199] Between 1983 and 1985, 270 cases of satanic abuse of children were reported in the United States and

---

[195] H. L. Kuhlmeyer, "Letter to McMartin Preschool Parents from Police Chief Kuhlmeyer," (September 8, 1983). https://goo.by/XAkYBb.

[196] Nathan and Snedeker, *Satan's Silence*, pp. 141–2.

[197] Victor, "Satanic Cult Rumors As Contemporary Legend," p. 69.

[198] P. Eberle, *The Abuse of Innocence: The McMartin Preschool Trial* (New York: Prometheus Books, 1993), pp. 172–3; R. Reinhold, "The Longest Trial – A Post-Mortem; Collapse of Child-Abuse Case: So Much Agony for So Little," *New York Times* (January 24, 1990). https://goo.by/NQHzfl; Nathan and Snedeker, *Satan's Silence*, p. 127.

[199] Beck, *We Believe the Children*, p. 81.

Canada.[200] Similar cases occurred in the United Kingdom and Australia. By some estimates, the victims of false accusations of SRA number in the thousands worldwide.[201] Meanwhile, the panic drew resources away from investigating actual cases of child abuse.

Several researchers have tried to explain why daycare providers were so often accused of being Satanists. Journalist Debbie Nathan and attorney Michael Snedecker interpreted the panic as a way of talking about family and sexual issues. There was a growing awareness of the problem of child abuse combined with resistance to what President Nixon called "communal approaches" to child rearing. Nathan and Snedecker suggest the nation was torn between the realization that children were being abused and a conservative desire to keep families sovereign from government interference. The SRA narratives became popular because they provided a way of talking about abuse while attributing its cause to a conspiracy of evil outsiders rather than parents and guardians.[202]

Sociologist David Bromley adds another insight regarding the suspicion of daycare providers. Economic changes in the 1980s had made two-income families the norm. Many parents were now forced to rely on daycare providers, bus drivers, and other strangers to raise their children. This situation may have *felt* like a conspiracy to corrupt their children and SRA narratives provided a way of expressing this frustration. As Bromley stated, "Satanism claims may be metaphorically true even if empirically false."[203]

The Murder of Mark Kilroy

The murder of University of Texas student Mark Kilroy (1966–89) became a seminal moment of the Satanic Panic. Kilroy disappeared while visiting the Mexican border town of Matamoros during spring break in 1989. His remains were later discovered on a ranch used by a drug cartel led by Adolfo de Jesús Constanzo (1962–89). Remains of fourteen others were found at the ranch, who had been killed between May 1988 and March 1989. These victims were police officers, rivals, and traitors whom the cartel deemed it necessary to murder. Kilroy was different: Constanzo practiced an idiosyncratic form of Afro-Cuban religion and cartel members testified that Constanzo ordered them to murder a random victim as a human sacrifice to bring the cartel supernatural aid.[204]

Mexican media immediately described the cartel as *narcosatanicos*. In the United States, claims makers declared this a smoking gun that proved organized

[200] Introvigne, *Satanism*, p. 406.

[201] J. S. Victor, "Crime, Moral Panic, and the Occult," in Christopher Partridge (ed.), *The Occult World* (New York: Routledge, 2014), pp. 692–700 (p. 694).

[202] Nathan and Snedeker, *Satan's Silence*.   [203] Bromley, "Satanism," p. 68.

[204] Introvigne, *Satanism*, p. 450.

Satanists were conducting human sacrifices. However, Constanzo was not a Satanist. He was the son of Cuban immigrants and his ritual practice combined deviant forms of two Afro-Cuban religions: Santería and Palo Mayombe. More importantly, the cartel revealed that Constanzo drew inspiration for his crimes from the film *The Believers* (1987) about a Santería cult that performs human sacrifice. Folklorist Bill Ellis has called this connection an example of ostension in which a horror movie presenting a distorted and problematic portrayal of Santería created the very scenario it depicted.[205]

The West Memphis Three

Some of the last victims of the Satanic Panic were the so-called West Memphis Three, three teenage boys from West Memphis, Arkansas. On May 6, 1993, the bodies of three eight-year-old boys were discovered in a water-filled ditch in the woods. They had been stripped naked and bound with their own shoelaces. They also had wounds that appeared to be bite marks and parts of one boy's genitals were missing. Years later, forensic investigators determined that these wounds were caused by scavengers, most likely turtles. But at the time, law enforcement interpreted them as evidence of ritualistic murder.

Statistically, with homicide victims aged six to eleven, the most likely perpetrators are the parents or stepparents.[206] But law enforcement leapt to the assumption that these murders had been conducted by a satanic cult. West Memphis Police assigned the murders case number 93–05–0 666, a reference to Satanism.[207] On May 7, police interviewed Damian Echols, whom they suspected of cult activity. Echols wore black clothing and enjoyed heavy metal music. He had also spent some time in a psychiatric institution being treated for depression.[208] Police approached Vicki Hutchinson, who had been accused of stealing from her employer, and offered to have the charges against her dropped if she would help them get incriminating evidence on Echols. Hutchinson first tried to seduce Echols and get him to admit to participating in witchcraft while wearing a recording device. According to Hutchinson, Echols explained he only maintained a spooky image so that people would leave him in peace. Police claimed the recording she took was indecipherable and later declared it lost.[209] Next, Hutchinson was coaxed into making a statement that Echols had taken her

---

[205] Ellis, *Aliens, Ghosts, and Cults*, p. 162.

[206] H. N. Snyder and M. Sickmund, *Juvenile Offenders and Victims: 2006 National Report* (Washington, DC: Office of Juvenile Justice, 2006), p. 22.

[207] D. O. Linder, "The West Memphis Three Trials: An Account." (n.d.). Famous-Trials.com. https://famous-trials.com/westmemphis/2287-home.

[208] Victor, "Crime, Moral Panic, and the Occult," p. 698.

[209] T. Hackler, "Complete Fabrication" *Arkansas Times* (October 7, 2004). https://bit.ly/49n48lt.

to a witch's gathering called an esbat, where he had confessed to committing the murders. There were numerous inconsistencies in this story and in 2004, Hutchinson finally admitted it had been a "total fabrication."[210]

Police next turned to David Miskelley Jr., another teenager who had some association with Echols. In addition to being a minor, Miskelley had developmental disabilities and an IQ of 72. He was interrogated for twelve hours without a lawyer and falsely told he had failed a lie detector test. Finally, Miskelley falsely confessed that he, Echols, and sixteen-year-old Jason Baldwin had committed the murders. This allowed police to arrest the West Memphis Three.

Miskelley recanted his confession and it was deemed inadmissible in court, but it was leaked to the papers, where jurors read it anyway. The prosecution brought in occult crime expert Dale Griffis, who declared that almost every detail of the case had occult significance: the victims had been eight years old, and Griffis claimed eight is a witch's number. The fact that there were three victims was somehow also evidence of Satanism. In addition, Griffis testified that Satanists wear black T-shirts and Echols owned more than a dozen of them.[211] Despite the lack of any forensic evidence, all three defendants were convicted. Miskelley and Baldwin were sentenced to life in prison and Echols was sentenced to death.

This might have been the end of the story were it not for documentarians Joe Berlinger and Bruce Sinofsky. They had originally come to West Memphis to make a documentary about heartless teenage murderers, but quickly saw that the West Memphis Three were being treated unfairly. Their documentary *Paradise Lost* (1996) and its two sequels rallied national support for the West Memphis Three. Metallica and other heavy metal bands also worked to raise awareness of the case. In 2011, the West Memphis Three were able to enter an Alford plea, a legal mechanism in which the defendant pleads innocence but concedes the state has sufficient evidence to convict them. This arrangement legally protected the state of Arkansas from what is now widely seen as a miscarriage of justice. The West Memphis Three's sentences were commuted to time served and they were released. The actual murderer was never identified.

The End of the Satanic Panic?

By the early 1990s, the Satanic Panic was showing signs of abatement. In 1992, Lanning released a report showing no evidence for a satanic conspiracy. In

---

[210] Hackler, "Complete Fabrication."

[211] D. O. Linder, "The Damien Echols and Jason Baldwin Trial (February 28–March 18, 1994): Dale Griffis." Famous-Trials.com. https://famous-trials.com/westmemphis/2272-griffistestbaldwin.

1993, the British government reached the same conclusion. On December 12, 1995, Geraldo Rivera, who had hosted a sensationalized special about Satanism in 1988, hosted a program on CNBC about false accusations of child molestation. He stated, "I am convinced that I was terribly wrong and many innocent people were convicted and went to prison as a result. And I am equally positive [that the] 'Repressed Memory Therapy Movement' is also a bunch of crap!"[212]

But while researchers, journalists, and law enforcement grew more skeptical of satanic conspiracy theories, these stories remained part of modern folklore. In 1994, 70 percent of people surveyed for the women's magazine *Redbook* reported belief in abusive satanic cults. Thirty-two percent agreed with the statement, "The FBI and the police ignore evidence because they don't want to admit the cults exist," and 22 percent agreed that cult leaders use brainwashing to ensure that the victims would not tell.[213]

A 2012 study of legal cases found evidence suggesting allegations of Satanism still have a profound effect on juries and judges.[214] The mental health profession was reluctant to acknowledge the excesses of figures such as Braun and claims of SRA and repressed memories remain popular among some segments of the profession. In 1984, Braun and others founded the International Society for the Study of Trauma and Dissociation (ISSTD). The group still holds regular meetings and some of its members continue to encourage their patients to believe they are victims of the kind of ritual abuse depicted in *Michelle Remembers*.[215]

In the twenty-first century, widespread use of social media, combined with algorithms that encourage extremism and the weaponization of urban legends for political purposes, has fostered a new brand of satanic panic. The episode known as the Hampstead Hoax demonstrated that SRA claims remain alive and well. In 2014, Ella Draper, a resident of the affluent Hampstead community in North London, reported that her two children had been abused by their father, from whom Draper had been estranged for years. In a taped interview, Draper's children told police their father was part of a ring of satanic pedophiles who killed babies and drank their blood. Police searched the local school and church

---

[212] Quoted in Lewis, *Satanism Today*, p. 226.

[213] W. Kaminer, *Sleeping with Extra-Terrestrials: The Rise of Irrationalism and Perils of Piety* (New York: Vintage Books, 1999), p. 193.

[214] J. Reichert and J. T. Richardson, "Decline of a Moral Panic: A Psychological and Socio-legal Examination of the Current Status of Satanism," *Nova Religio* 16.2 (2012), 47–63.

[215] For critical reportage on an ISSTD meeting, see J. L. Flatley, *Satan Goes to the Mind Control Convention: Manchurian Candidates, Recovered Memories, and the Dark Side of Conspiracy Culture (and other stories)*. (ebook: Joseph L. Flatley Press, 2018). On ISSTD founder and former president Braun, see Noll, "When Psychiatry Battled the Devil." On lawsuits against former ISSTD president Colin Ross, see M. Jenkins, "American Therapy That Could Blow Your Minds," *Independent* (February 9, 1997). https://goo.by/COiwet.

for secret rooms where the children said babies were killed. No evidence was found. Eventually, the children confessed that they had been lying. Draper's current boyfriend, Abraham Christie, had pressured them into telling this story, abusing them if they did not comply.

No charges were filed and Draper continued to sue for custody of her children. She recruited Sabine McNeil, a conspiracy theorist, to help with her case. In January 2015, McNeil took confidential information from Draper's case – including videos of police interviews where children describe SRA – and uploaded it to the Internet. McNeil also published an eleven-page-document titled "Mass Child Sex Abuse in Satanic Ritual Abuse and Sacrifice Cult." It contained the names and personal information of 175 parents, teachers, and staff members connected to the Hampstead school that Draper's children attended and claimed they were satanic pedophiles. This material went viral online, promoted on websites run by prominent conspiracy theorists Alex Jones and David Icke. People on McNeil's list received death threats and feared vigilantes would kidnap their children. Some even received calls from actual pedophiles offering to pay for sex with their children. Draper fled the country after the judge in her case demanded an explanation. An army of volunteers worked to get the material off the Internet and collect data with which to charge McNeil for harassment. In 2019, McNeil was sentenced to nine years in prison.[216]

One year after the Hampstead Hoax, the so-called Pizzagate episode occurred in the United States. Presidential candidate Hillary Clinton's campaign's emails were hacked and posted online. A rumor started that Ping Pong Comet Pizza – a pizzeria in Washington, DC, referenced in the emails – was a front for satanic leaders of the Democratic Party and that the basement contained children who were being sexually abused. On December 4, 2016, Edgar Maddison Welch drove from North Carolina to Ping Pong Comet Pizza armed with an AR-15– style rifle and demanded to inspect the basement. He surrendered to authorities after discovering the restaurant had no basement.

In 2017, online claims about Satanism and the Democratic Party developed into a movement known as QAnon – named after an anonymous forum poster calling him or herself "Q" and falsely claiming to be a ranking intelligence officer with "Q-level clearance." QAnon followers claimed President Donald Trump was waging a covert war against a deep state that secretly runs the government and engages in child trafficking and SRA. They awaited an event called the Storm, in which Trump would round up and execute deep state operatives for their crimes, including Hillary Clinton. QAnon developed by

---

[216] A. Mostrous, "The Hampstead Sex Cult Hoax," *Daily Mail* (September 23, 2022). https://goo
.by/tNnDRp.

dropping vague clues online and leaving followers to expand these statements into conspiracy theories. Some game designers who studied QAnon noted that it resembled a calculated effort to gamify conspiracy theories in ways that would help far-right politicians win elections.[217]

In February 2022, Russia invaded Ukraine. After Ukraine put up unexpected resistance, Russian leader Vladimir Putin was pressured to justify his war. In October, Russian officials began claiming the purpose of the war was to de-Satanize Ukraine and that the United States was actively working to introduce Satanism to Russia. This propaganda campaign was likely directed not only at the Russian people, but at Americans as well. Putin may have hoped to use satanic conspiracy theories to help far-right Republicans win in midterm elections, which would make it more difficult for President Joe Biden to send weapons and supplies to Ukraine. A *Washington Post* reporter observed, "The Kremlin is trying to align with U.S. 'Satanic panic.'"[218] Propaganda such as this demonstrates that the Satanic Panic of the 1980s never ended. In fact, it is arguably more dangerous than ever now that claims made online can acquire a global audience and political extremists have begun to use satanic conspiracy theories as a tool for achieving their goals.

7 Contemporary Developments in Satanism

Satanism is once again having a moment in the spotlight. While Satanism remains a tiny minority religion compared to traditions like Christianity and Islam, there are more Satanists today than ever before and they have exerted an organized presence in the public square. Several factors contributed to this renewed popularity of Satanism. One factor is the Satanic Panic itself. Many people currently leading satanic organizations are members of Generation X who grew up being told adolescent pastimes like rock music or the game *Dungeons and Dragons* are satanic. Now adults, they view Satanism as a useful tool for expressing their rejection of conservative Christian hegemony. Another factor is the advent of social media and online print-on-demand services, which have made it incredibly easy for anyone forming a new satanic organization to create an online presence and publish books. However, in the United States, the biggest factor appears to be a culture war fueled by demographic changes. Experiments in Satanism seem to arise when a culture feels itself at a crossroads. The rise of the CoS in 1966 reflected a metaphysical crossroads

---

[217] R. Berkowitz, "QAnon Resembles the Games I Design. But for Believers, There Is No Winning," *The Washington Post* (May 11, 2021). www.washingtonpost.com/outlook/qanon-game-plays-believers/2021/05/10/31d8ea46-928b-11eb-a74e-1f4cf89fd948_story.html.

[218] C. Sirikupt, "Russia Now Says It Must 'de-Satanize' Ukraine. What?" *The Washington Post* (November 17, 2022). https://goo.by/TusMqr.

when America felt torn between materialism and science, its religious past and its anticipated secular future. The current wave of political Satanism reflects a different crossroads where America is divided between nostalgia for a whiter, more Christian, less secular country, and hope for a religiously plural nation where church and state remain separate.

According to a Pew Research Center report, the number of Americans who identify as Christian has shrunk to only 63 percent, while those identifying with no religion has risen to 29 percent.[219] Robert P. Jones of the Public Religion Research Institute has suggested that America's Christian establishment is alarmed about this shift and has tried to compensate for the loss of demographic power by using the power of the state. This is why, in recent years, there have been efforts to erect monuments of the Ten Commandments at state capitols or otherwise use government institutions to signal the cultural dominance of Christianity. Donald Trump became president in 2016 by using his slogan of "Make America Great Again," signaling to many a promise to return to a white, Christian America. In return for electing him, Trump delivered three conservative justices to the Supreme Court, who in 2022, overturned the *Roe* v. *Wade* decision that made abortion a Constitutional right. Many on the political left, particularly among the 29 percent who identify as having no religion, have responded to this situation by declaring themselves Satanists.

One consequence of this development is that Satanism has, on the whole, become much more openly political and progressive then in the period between 1966 and 2013. The Satanic Temple (TST) is a left-wing satanic organization founded in 2013 that has taken a stance on such issues as the separation of church and state, reproductive rights, and transgender rights. It also engages in philanthropy such as caring for the homeless, adopting beaches and highways, and working to inform the public about mental health professionals who continue to promote claims of SRA. It has also created an alternative program to Alcoholics Anonymous.

Progressivism has even infiltrated satanic music, which has historically celebrated nihilism. Twin Temple is a satanic doo-wop band whose act combines satanic ritual and chalices filled with blood with musical progressions reminiscent of the 1950s. Married duo Alexandra and Zachary James allegedly formed their band after performing a satanic destruction ritual on Halloween 2016. Alexandra's description of their fans reflects the demographic changes described by Jones: "We've had a lot of women, members of the LGBTQ

---

[219] G. A. Smith, "About Three-in-Ten U.S. Adults Are Now Religiously Unaffiliated," Pew Research Center (December 14, 2021). https://goo.by/kosYoG.

community, people of colour and people who just feel like outsiders tell us they love our message of inclusion."[220]

This wave of kinder, more progressive Satanism has resulted in some gate-keeping from the larger satanic milieu. Some want Satanism to remain sinister and frightening and resent the positivity of newer Satanists. The CoS maintains its position that they are the only true Satanists and have expressed contempt for TST, with whom they are frequently confused by the media. The CoS has historically advocated a position of conservative libertarianism in contrast to TST, which emphasizes social justice and empathy. There are also groups like the ONA and Joy of Satan that explicitly endorse far-right extremism.

Despite this pushback, the long view of Satanism looks more progressive than LaVey's writings might suggest. Lewis ran a series of global survey studies of Satanists between 2000 and 2011. At least at the global level, he found Satanists tended to lean progressive on issues of individual liberty such as abortion and LGBTQ rights. But they also tended to support social welfare, including government funding for childcare, healthcare, higher education, and unemployment benefits. He concluded, "In sum, this sample consisted mostly of people that conservative American politicians would label 'Socialists.' . . . It also stands in sharp contrast with the social Darwinism advocated by LaVey."[221] It should be recalled that the Romantics who reformed the image of Satan tended to be progressives who championed liberty and reason. In this sense, Satanism may be returning to its roots.

The Satanic Temple

The Satanic Temple is currently the most prominent satanic organization in terms of both size and public activity. The two individuals most involved in its founding are known as Doug Mesner and Malcolm Jarry. The pair met at Harvard University in 2012 where they had both been students. In March of that year, Governor Rick Scott of Florida signed a bill allowing public school students to read inspirational messages at assemblies and sporting events. The apparent goal of the bill was to get around the Supreme Court's ruling that mandatory prayer in school is a violation of the Establishment Clause. Jarry decided to conduct an experiment for a paper he was writing: He would organize a rally of Satanists praising Rick Scott for his new law because it would allow satanic students to use public schools to share their love of Satan.

---

[220] J. Selzer, "Twin Temple Are the Satanic Doo-wop Duo Metal Fans Have Embraced," Loudersound.com (December 18, 2020). https://goo.by/KIdcDa.

[221] Dyrendal, Lewis, and Petersen, *Invention of Satanism*, p. 175.

The rally was held on December 25, 2013. Jarry hired actors to play members of TST. Mesner, who had some background with the CoS, helped as a consultant on Satanism. At the rally, he identified himself as Lucien Greaves, which became his TST persona. Parts of the rally can be seen in the documentary *Hail Satan?* (2019), directed by Penny Lane. It is absurd and funny to watch, but Jarry insisted that it was a political action, not just a prank. He wanted to see whether the public would show any understanding that the separation of church and state is good for everyone, not just non-Christians.

The rally might have been the end of TST, but on April 13, 2013, adolescent Muslim terrorists bombed the Boston Marathon. Westboro Baptist Church sought to capitalize on this tragedy by picketing the funerals of the victims. Jarry and Mesner, who lived in Boston, decided to go on the offensive against the Westboro Baptist Church. In July 2013, they drove to Meridian, Mississippi, where the mother of the church's founder, Fred Phelps, is buried. They arranged to have gay couples kiss over the grave and announced that this was part of satanic ritual called a pink mass that had turned Fred Phelp's mother gay in the afterlife. Pictures of the pink mass became a sensation, in part because Westboro Baptist Church is almost universally hated. The Satanic Temple was now known around the country.

As the movement became more serious, Jarry and Mesner composed the Seven Tenets, a statement meant to articulate their sincerely held beliefs:

1. One should strive to act with compassion and empathy toward all creatures in accordance with reason.
2. The struggle for justice is an ongoing and necessary pursuit that should prevail over laws and institutions.
3. One's body is inviolable, subject to one's own will alone.
4. The freedoms of others should be respected, including the freedom to offend. To willfully and unjustly encroach upon the freedoms of another is to forgo one's own.
5. Beliefs should conform to one's best scientific understanding of the world. One should take care never to distort scientific facts to fit one's beliefs.
6. People are fallible. If one makes a mistake, one should do one's best to rectify it and resolve any harm that might have been caused.
7. Every tenet is a guiding principle designed to inspire nobility in action and thought. The spirit of compassion, wisdom, and justice should always prevail over the written or spoken word.

Significantly, Satan is not mentioned explicitly anywhere in these tenets. Like the CoS, TST regards Satan as a symbol that embodies their values of liberty and self-determination. This has led some critics to claim that TST is not really a religion, but a political movement or a prank. On the other hand, TST has no scientific argument for why the pursuit of justice and compassion should be guiding principles for one's life. This is regarded as self-evident or – drawing the comparison with other religions – a matter of faith. Many who joined TST described how the Seven Tenets resonated with them and in, a sense, sacralized the values they already had.[222]

The Satanic Temple began its next major project in December 2013. In 2012, a monument to the Ten Commandments was erected at the Oklahoma state capitol – an action that the Oklahoma Supreme Court later ruled violated the state constitution. Oklahoma's bill proposing the monument was inspired by the Supreme Court case *Van Orden* v. *Perry* (2005), which ruled that a similar monument at the Texas capitol was constitutional because surrounding monuments created a context that somehow changed its meaning to something other than a direct government endorsement of Christianity. Accordingly, Oklahoma's bill called for the eventual creation of other monuments at the capitol to create a context in which a Ten Commandments monument could legally be claimed to be a secular symbol. Jarry and Mesner offered to help by donating a statue of Satan to be erected next the Ten Commandments. Like many of TST's provocations, the message behind this offer was clear: The government must either not endorse Christianity or endorse all religions, including Satanism.

Their proposal was considered outrageous and received national attention. More than $30,000 was donated to construct the statue, which eventually cost more than $100,000. The monument – named Baphomet with Children – is a bronze statue resembling Baphomet as drawn by Lévi flanked by two adoring children. It is more than seven feet tall and weighs approximately 3,000 pounds. Unlike Lévi's original drawing, TST's Baphomet lacks female breasts so that the state legislature could not disqualify it on grounds of obscenity. The statue had no direct effect on the Oklahoma Supreme Court's decision to have the Ten Commandments removed. However, when there was discussion of simply amending the state constitution so that government resources could be used to endorse specific religions, some Oklahoma journalists warned that this could eventually lead to TST erecting their statue to Satan.

The situation in Oklahoma repeated itself in Arkansas, where another Ten Commandments monument was installed and, once again, TST offered to complement it with their Baphomet monument. In 2016, Lucien Greaves met with the Arkansas State Capitol Arts and Grounds Commission to discuss installing Baphomet. Then the legislature passed a new law declaring the situation an emergency and announcing retroactively that all such proposals must first be

---

[222] Laycock, *Speak of the Devil*, p. 38. The Seven Tenets can be viewed at https://t.ly/ZsAG7.

reviewed by the legislature. The Satanic Temple sued on the grounds of religious discrimination. Their case, as well as a case filed by the ACLU over Arkansas's Ten Commandments monument, are still ongoing. The Baphomet statue currently resides at TST's headquarters in Salem, Massachusetts.[223]

Not long after the construction of the Baphomet statue, TST began to form local chapters throughout the United States as well as in Canada and Europe, becoming a full-fledged new religious movement. Chapters – later renamed congregations – met regularly to socialize, hold book clubs, and engage in philanthropy. They began holding rituals they had devised, including black masses and unbaptisms. Sometimes these rituals were private, sometimes they were events open to the public that served to raise money for TST's growing number of lawsuits. The daily activities and shared values of these communities is probably the greatest evidence that TST is now a religion rather than a prank or a political stunt.

As is common with NRMs, especially those undergoing rapid growth, the group's organizational structure changed rapidly. Several chapters became frustrated and defected to form their own groups. As is also common with NRMs, some former members expressed bitterness toward their former organization and condemned it as a cult. Significantly, though, most former TST members did not renounce Satanism or political activism. If anything, they claimed they could continue to do this kind of work even better without TST.

In 2019, the IRS granted TST tax-exempt status as a church. With this move, it became significantly more difficult for the group's opponents to legally claim it was not actually a religion. The Satanic Temple has continued to launch campaigns, most of which focus around two goals. First, as with the controversy over the Baphomet statue, TST continues to demand that Satanism be given the same privilege and access to government institutions that Christianity enjoys. Second, as the Supreme Court has expanded the idea of religious liberty, TST has demanded religious exemption from laws that violate members' sincerely held religious beliefs, notably restrictions on abortion. Both goals are intended to place a check on Christian nationalism by forcing a choice: either separate church and state or be prepared to see Satanists in the public square enjoying religious privileges.

Regarding the first goal, TST has erected displays at time at state capitols and other government properties to exist alongside other displays. In cities that begin city council meetings with prayer invocations, TST has sued to give satanic prayers. Several cities have found loopholes that allow them to legally

---

[223] D. Ellis, "State, Satanic Temple Ask for Judgment in Ten Commandments Case," *Arkansas Democrat Gazette* (March 8, 2023). https://bit.ly/3SkTxl9.

host Christian prayers while excluding Satanists. Phoenix, Arizona, changed its policy so that only police and fire chaplains may give prayers and Boston's rule is that any clergy must be invited by a city council member.[224]

The Satanic Temple's most controversial endeavor on this front has been to hold satanic education for young children in public schools. This is in response to a Supreme Court ruling that the Good News Club, a Christian ministry aimed at children, must be allowed the use of public school facilities after school, unless all outside groups are denied such access. The Satanic Temple's answer to this was the Afterschool Satan Club (ASSC). Despite the name, the ASSC's curriculum emphasizes learning about science, critical thinking, and anti-bullying rather than religious doctrines. The Satanic Temple began petitioning for their club to meet at schools that host a chapter of the Good News Club. The program faced numerous setbacks: few parents were willing to sign children up for the program, insurance companies refused to contract with TST, and schools often stonewalled by refusing to communicate with TST or inventing red tape to stymie requests. In schools where ASSC clubs were approved, Christian parents threatened to withdraw their children from school and accused superintendents of being Satanists. When an ASSC club was approved at Saucon Valley Middle School in Pennsylvania in 2023, twenty-year-old Ceu Uk of North Carolina called the school and threatened, "I'm going to come in there and shoot everybody," causing the school to temporarily close.[225]

Regarding the second goal, TST has initiated a number of campaigns based around its third tenet that one's body is inviolable. These campaigns were inspired by the Supreme Court decision *Burwell* v. *Hobby Lobby* (2014), which ruled that the Green family's Christian beliefs rendered their company, Hobby, Lobby, exempt from compliance with parts of the Affordable Care Act. The Satanic Temple began seeking similar exemptions for satanic beliefs. In 2014, TST announced its Protect Children Project, which took aim at public schools that still practiced corporal punishment. The Satanic Temple argued that students with a sincere religious belief that one's body is inviolable should be legally exempt from such punishment.

The Satanic Temple has also claimed that the third tenet should grant them a religious exemption from state restrictions on abortion. Beginning in 2015, TST filed a series of lawsuits against the state of Missouri, which required

---

[224] Jonah Hicap, "Phoenix City Council Brings Back Prayer to Public Meetings – but Limited to Fire, Police Chaplains," *Christian Today* (March 14, 2016). https://goo.by/zHKYxa; "Satanic Temple Suit over Boston Council Prayer Moves Forward," Associated Press (July 23, 2021). https://goo.by/RnMjTO.

[225] J. Popichak, "DA: Man Angered by 'After School Satan Club' Said He'd 'Shoot Everybody,'" *Saucon Source* (February 28, 2013). https://goo.by/LSZYVE.

a woman seeking an abortion to visit the state's only provider, read an informed consent booklet, then return seventy-two hours later if they still sought an abortion. The booklet stated, "The life of each human being begins at conception. Abortion will terminate the life of a separate, unique, living human being." The Satanic Temple argued that such a claim amounted to a government endorsement of Christianity and that the law violated their religious beliefs. The Satanic Temple's cases were dismissed on procedural grounds without answering whether Satanists had a legal right to exemption from these restrictions. In one case, a judge waited more than nine months to try the case then ruled that the plaintiff – a satanic woman seeking an abortion – did not have standing to sue because she was no longer pregnant. In 2020, TST created a satanic abortion ritual, which involves a woman affirming her own autonomy and is not completed until she has received her abortion. In theory, this increased the burden that states like Missouri put on Satanism because their restrictions are directly interfering with a religious practice. Pro-life critics naturally cited this as evidence that Satanists regard abortion itself as sacred, akin to human sacrifice. For TST, it is a variation on the destruction ritual created by LaVey, aimed at destroying feelings of doubt and guilt.

In 2022, The Supreme Court, led by conservative Justice Samuel Alito, struck down *Roe* v. *Wade*, freeing states to completely ban abortion. In 2023, TST opened its own clinic, the Samuel Alito's Mom's Satanic Abortion Clinic, in New Mexico, a state where abortion access is relatively protected. The clinic provides telemedicine for New Mexico residents seeking an abortion and mails packages containing abortion-inducing medication, medication to manage the side effects, and pregnancy tests. The clinic also offers resources for those who cannot afford medication or travel to New Mexico.

Public Satanism

While TST generated the most headlines in the past ten years, Satanists of all stripes have been increasingly open about their presence, often to the alarm of their Christian neighbors. Adam Daniels of Oklahoma City is a theistic Satanist who organized a series of public satanic rituals between 2010 and 2016, held at the Oklahoma City Civic Center. On September 21, 2014, he held a black mass that drew 1,600 Catholic protestors led by Archbishop Paul Coakley. Daniels consistently claimed these performances were acts of resistance against an unjust Christian majority and "enslavement by the Catholic Church."[226]

---

[226] M. Patterson, "Satanists Planning Christmas Eve Display in Oklahoma City," NewsOK.com (December 11, 2015). https://goo.by/zBjYBl.

In 2015, the Greater Church of Lucifer acquired a building on Main Street in Spring, Texas. The church is led by Michael W. Ford and his wife, Hope Marie Ford. They have described their tradition as Luciferian witchcraft. Their group had previously existed online and many members planned to meet each other in person for the first time at the grand opening to be held on October 30, 2015. The town of Spring responded with threats and vandalism. The opening was met with scores of protestors, many of them from out of state.

Before Christmas 2016, in Boca Raton, Florida, Preston Smith, an atheist who taught language arts at a local middle school, became frustrated that a public park had been declared an open forum so that sectarian Christmas displays could be erected. In response, Smith acquired a permit to erect a ten-foot-tall red pentagram he had constructed out of aluminum, weighing 300 pounds. Messages on Smith's monument read "In Satan We Trust" and "May the Children Hail Satan." The Liberty Counsel, a conservative Christian legal group, took aim at Smith's employers, demanding the school district turn over any emails by Smith containing the words "Satan," "Christian," or "atheism."[227] As in Spring, Texas, vandals repeatedly damaged the display, with one person dragging it with a truck, destroying the park's lawn in the process.

As Satanists seek to take a place in the public square alongside Christianity, they are also forcing a larger conversation about what constitutes a religion and what religious freedom looks like in practice. Confronted with the possibility of having to coexist with Satanists, some Americans attempted to revise the definition of the First Amendment or even renounced religious freedom altogether. In response to Preston Smith, one Boca Raton paster claimed the Constitution only applies to "traditional, accepted religions like Christianity" and not to "malevolent and evil faiths like Satanism."[228] Christine Weick – famous for a conspiracy theory that the logo for Monster energy drink contains satanic imagery – joined protestors in Spring, Texas, and told a reporter, "This is what we get when we have freedom of religion."[229]

Satanism appears to be on the rise in other countries as well. The Satanic Temple has had chapters in several European countries, and people from Africa and South America have expressed interest in creating chapters. However, in addition to the usual difficulties in keeping a satanic organization together,

---

[227] L. Ramadan, "Two Boca Raton Schools Become Battle Ground for Religious Debate," *Palm Beach Post* (January 4, 2017). https://goo.by/GxcLbv.

[228] D. Ferguson, "Florida Pastor: First Amendment Doesn't Apply to 'Malevolent, Evil' Faiths Like Satanism," *Rawstory.com* (December 18, 2014). https://bit.ly/46WzNsz.

[229] "Protest and Prayer Fill Air Outside Greater Church of Lucifer," ABC13.com (October 30, 2015). https://goo.by/XwetZC.

TST's interests and tactics were uniquely adapted to the American Constitution. Former TST members in the United Kingdom formed the Global Order of Satan, which sought to incorporate other international chapters. They have taken on a number of issues, such as petition campaigns urging European nations to ban conversion therapy intended to change the sexual orientation of LGBTQ people.[230] In 2019, Trevor Bell and Robin Bristow of Queensland, Australia, founded the Noosa Temple of Satan and demanded they be allowed to offer religious instruction about Satanism in primary schools. Their proposal was rejected and the Queensland Supreme Court ruled that their group did not meet the legal criteria for a religious organization.[231] In 2020, the South African Satanic Church (SASC) was founded by LaVeyan Satanists Riaan Swiegelaar and Adri Norton and opened a physical office in Cape Town. However, in July 2022, Swiegelaar announced that he had converted to Christianity, causing the SASC to become moribund. Satanic panic remains a potent force in South African culture and Swiegelaar began giving seminars promising to expose Satanism. This led some Satanists to speculate that he had helped create the SASC with the intention of propping up a lucrative career as an ex-Satanist.[232] Satanism has also had a burgeoning presence in Japan. This is somewhat surprising as Japan is not a historically Christian country. However, journalist La Carmina notes that Japanese culture demands a high degree of conformity and this makes Satanism appealing as an outlet for transgression and freedom.[233]

It is impossible to predict the future of the satanic milieu. However, in the short run, Satanism seems to be gaining popularity, becoming more progressive and more acceptable. This may drive left-hand path groups that have conservative values or that seek a truly sinister reputation to move further away from Satanism. It also seems that as nontheistic groups like TST continue to demand constitutional rights, there will be growing awareness that religion is not synonymous with belief in the supernatural. For many Satanists, the values of freedom and self-determination, as celebrated by their tradition, are as valid a faith as any other.

---

[230] "Global Order of Satan." www.globalorderofsatan.com.

[231] P. Doneman and T. Siganto, "Noosa Temple of Satan Education Challenge Dismissed by Judge as 'Jumble of Confected Nonsense.'" ABC.net.au (May 7, 2022). https://bit.ly/40iYMDX.

[232] C. Engela, "What Happened to the South African Satanic Church? . . . And Other Unanswered Questions," *Christina Engela: Author* (March 11, 2023). https://bit.ly/40ChNS1.

[233] La Carmina, *Little Book of Satanism*, p. 133.

Bibliography

"8/8/88 Rally: Radio Werewolf, Boyd Rice, Zeena Schreck, Adam Parfrey." www.youtube.com/watch?v=vx0kRUOzrxI.

Aberjonois, F. "Witches Reported Active in Toledo." *Toledo Blade* (December 2, 1968), 1.

Adler, J., and P. Abramson. "The Second Beast of Revelation." *Newsweek* (November 16, 1987), 73.

Alfred, R. H. "The Church of Satan." In J. R. Lewis and J. A. Petersen (eds.), *The Encyclopedic Sourcebook of Satanism*. Amherst, NY: Prometheus Books, 2008, pp. 478–502.

Aquino, M. *The Church of Satan* vol. I. 8th ed. Michael Aquino, 2013.

Baddeley, G. *Lucifer Rising*. London: Plexus, 1999.

Barton, B. *The Secret Life of a Satanist: The Authorized Biography of Anton LaVey*. Los Angeles, CA: Feral House, 1990.

Beck, R. *We Believe the Children: A Moral Panic in the 1980s*. New York: PublicAffairs 2015.

Ben-Yehuda, N. *Deviance and Moral Boundaries: Witchcraft, the Occult, Science Fiction, Deviant Sciences, and Scientists*. Chicago, IL: University of Chicago Press, 1985.

Berkowitz, R. "QAnon Resembles the Games I Design: But for Believers, There Is No Winning." *The Washington Post* (May 11, 2021). bit.ly/49lwjS4.

Boulware, J. "A Devil of a Time." *The Washington Post* (August 30, 1998). wapo.st/40nW4gb.

Bromley, D. G. "Satanism: The New Cult Scare." In J. T. Richardson, J. Best, and D. G. Bromley (eds.), *The Satanism Scare*. Hawthorne, NY: Aldine De Gruyter, 1991, pp. 49–74.

Church of Satan. "Satan Wants You!" (n.d.). https://bit.ly/3Sv8npn.

Davies, O. *Grimoires: A History of Magic Books*. Oxford: Oxford University Press, 2009.

Doneman, P., and T. Siganto. "Noosa Temple of Satan Education Challenge Dismissed by Judge As 'Jumble of Confected Nonsense.'" ABC.net.au (May 7, 2022). https://bit.ly/40iYMDX.

Dyrendal, A. "Satan and the Beast: The Influence of Aleister Crowley on Modern Satanism." In H. Bogdan and M. P. Starr, eds., *Aleister Crowley and Western Esotericism*. New York: Oxford University Press, 2012, pp. 369–94.

Dyrendal, A., J. R. Lewis, and J. A. Petersen. *The Invention of Satanism.* New York: Oxford University Press, 2015.

Eberle, P. *The Abuse of Innocence: The McMartin Preschool Trial.* New York: Prometheus Books, 1993.

Ellis, B. *Aliens, Ghosts, and Cults: Legends We Live.* Jackson: University Press of Mississippi, 2003.

Ellis, D. "State, Satanic Temple Ask for Judgment in Ten Commandments Case," *Arkansas Democrat Gazette* (March 8, 2023). https://bit.ly/3SkTxl9.

Engela, C. "What Happened to the South African Satanic Church? ... And Other Unanswered Questions." Christinaengela.com (March 11, 2023). https://bit.ly/40ChNS1.

"Evil, Anyone?" *Newsweek* (August 16, 1971). p. 56.

Faxneld, P. *Satanic Feminism: Lucifer As the Liberator of Woman in Nineteenth-Century Culture.* New York: Oxford University Press, 2017.

Faxneld, P. "The Strange Case of Ben Kadosh: A Luciferian Pamphlet from 1906 and Its Current Renaissance." *Aries* 11 (2011), 1–22.

Faxneld, P. "Witches, Anarchism, and Evolutionism: Stanislaw Przybyszewski's Fin-de-siècle Satanism and the Demonic Feminine." In P. Faxneld and J. A. Petersen (eds.), *The Devil's Party: Satanism in Modernity.* New York: Oxford University Press, 2012, pp. 53–78.

Faxneld, P., and J. A. Petersen. "Part Two: The Black Pope and the Church of Satan." In P. Faxneld and J. A. Petersen (eds.), *The Devil's Party: Satanism in Modernity.* New York: Oxford University Press, 2013, pp. 80–3.

Federal Bureau of Investigation (FBI). "Freedom of Information Act/Privacy Acts Release – Subject: Anton LaVey." https://bit.ly/46VxhTk.

Ferguson, D. "Florida Pastor: First Amendment Doesn't Apply to 'Malevolent, Evil' Faiths Like Satanism." Rawstory.com (December 18, 2014). https://bit.ly/46WzNsz.

Fishgall, G. *Gonna Do Great Things: The Life of Sammy Davis, Jr.* New York: Scribner, 2003.

Flatley, J. L. *Satan Goes to the Mind Control Convention: Manchurian Candidates, Recovered Memories, and the Dark Side of Conspiracy Culture (and Other Stories).* Philadelphia, PA: Joseph L. Flatley Press, 2018.

Flowers, S. E. *Lords of the Left-Hand Path: A History of Spiritual Dissent.* 2nd ed. Smithville, TX: Runa-Raven Press, 1997.

Foertsch, S. "An Organizational Analysis of the Schismatic Church of Satan." *Review of Religious Research* 64 (2022), 55–76.

Frankfurter, D. "Awakening to Satanic Conspiracy: *Rosemary's Baby* and the Cult Next Door." In M. D. Eckel and B. L. Herling (eds.), *Deliver Us from*

Evil. Boston University Studies in Philosophy and Religion. New York: Continuum, 2011, pp. 75–86.

Frankfurter, D. *Evil Incarnate: Rumors of Demonic Conspiracy and Satanic Abuse in History*. Princeton, NJ: Princeton University Press, 2006.

Gardner, G. *Witchcraft Today*. New York: Kensington, 2004.

Gault, M. "FBI Bankrolled Publisher of Occult Neo-Nazi Books, Feds Claim." Vice.com (August 25, 2021). https://bit.ly/3tUtLdf.

Gilmore, P. H. "Regarding Herbert A. Sloane and His Affiliation with the Church of Satan." ChurchofSatan.com (July 22, 2018). www.churchofsa tan.com/regarding-herbert-a-sloane.

Gilmore, P. H. "Yes, We Have No Occultism." ChurchofSatan.com (n.d.). www .churchofsatan.com/yes-we-have-no-occultism.

"Global Order of Satan." www.globalorderofsatan.com.

Goodrick-Clarke, N. *Black Sun: Aryan Cults Esoteric Nazism and the Politics of Identity*. New York: New York University Press, 2002.

Graham, H. "Satanism in Britain Today." *Journal of Contemporary Religion* 10.3 (1995), 283–96.

Granholm, K. "Embracing Others Than Satan: The Multiple Princes of Darkness in the Left-Hand Path Milieu." In J. A. Petersen (ed.), *Contemporary Religious Satanism: A Critical Anthology*. New York: Routledge, 2016, pp. 85–102.

Granholm, K. "The Left-Hand Path and Post-Satanism: The Temple of Set and the Evolution of Satanism." In P. Faxneld and J. A. Petersen (eds.), *The Devil's Party: Satanism in Modernity*. New York: Oxford University Press, 2013, pp. 209–28.

Griffin, A. C., and L. E. Milano. "Hatred at Harvard." *The Harvard Crimson* (May 12, 2014). www.thecrimson.com/article/2014/5/12/hatred-at-harvard.

Gumaer, D. E. "Satanism: A Practical Guide to Witch-Hunting," *American Opinion* 13.8 (September 1970), 41–8.

Hackler, T. "Complete Fabrication." *Arkansas Times* (October 7, 2004). https:// bit.ly/49n48lt.

Hanson, C. "Dangerous Therapy: The Story of Patricia Burgus and Multiple Personality Disorder." *Chicago* (June 1, 1998). https://bit.ly/3sr1U3Q.

Harrington, W. "The Devil in Anton LaVey." *The Washington Post* Magazine (February 23, 1986), 7.

Harvey, G. "Satanism in Britain Today." *Journal of Contemporary Religion* 10.3 (1995), 283–96.

Hernandez, A. "Satanic Panic in Colorado." Denverlibrary.org (December 7, 2021). https://history.denverlibrary.org/news/satanic-panic.

Hicap, J. "Phoenix City Council Brings Back Prayer to Public Meetings: But Limited to Fire, Police Chaplains." *Christian Today* (March 14, 2016). https://goo.by/zHKYxa.

Hicks, R. *In Pursuit of Satan: The Police and the Occult.* Buffalo, NY: Prometheus Books, 1991.

Introvigne, M. *Satanism: A Social History.* Leiden: Brill, 2016.

Jenkins, M. "American Therapy That Could Blow Your Minds." *Independent* (February 9, 1997). https://goo.by/COiwet.

Kahaner, L. *Cults That Kill: Probing the Underworld of Occult Crime.* New York: Warner Books, 1988.

Kaminer, W. *Sleeping with Extra-Terrestrials: The Rise of Irrationalism and Perils of Piety.* New York: Vintage Books, 1999.

Klein, K. "Witches Are Back and So Are Satanists." *The Washington Post* (May 10, 1970), 10.

Kluft, R. P. "Reflections on Allegations of Ritual Abuse." *Dissociation* 3.4 (December 1989), 191–3.

Kuhlmeyer, H. L. "Letter to McMartin Preschool Parents from Police Chief Kuhlmeyer" (September 8, 1983). https://goo.by/XAkYBb.

La Carmina, *The Little Book of Satanism: A Guide to Satanic History, Culture, and Wisdom.* Berkeley, CA: Ulysses Press, 2022.

Lanning, K. V. "Investigator's Guide to Allegations of 'Ritual' Child Abuse." Washington, DC: FBI/US Department of Justice, 1992.

LaVey, A. S. "The Eleven Satanic Rules of the Earth" (1967). www.churchofsatan.com/eleven-rules-of-earth.

LaVey, A. S. "The Nine Satanic Sins" (1987). www.churchofsatan.com/nine-satanic-sins.

LaVey, A. S. "Pentagonal Revisionism: A Five-Point Program" (1988). www.churchofsatan.com/pentagonal-revisionism.

LaVey, A. S. *Satan Speaks!* Portland, OR: Feral House, 1998.

LaVey, A. S. *The Satanic Bible.* New York: Avon, 1969.

LaVey, A. S. *The Satanic Rituals.* New York: Avon, 1972.

Laycock, J. P. *Speak of the Devil: How the Satanic Temple Is Changing the Way We Talk about Religion.* New York: Oxford University Press, 2020.

Lewis, J. R. *Legitimating New Religions.* New Brunswick, NJ: Rutgers University Press, 2003.

Lewis, J. R. *Satanism Today: An Encyclopedia of Religion, Folklore, and Popular Culture.* Santa Barbara, CA: ABC–CLIO, 2002.

Linder, D. O. "The Damien Echols and Jason Baldwin Trial (February 28–March 18, 1994): Dale Griffis." Famous-Trials.com. https://famous-trials.com/westmemphis/2272-griffistestbaldwin.

Linder, D. O. "The West Memphis Three Trials: An Account." (n.d.). Famous-Trials.com. https://famous-trials.com/westmemphis/2287-home.

Lord, E. *Hellfire Clubs: Sex, Satanism and Secret Societies*. New Haven, CT: Yale University Press 2010.

Lyons, A. *Satan Wants You: The Cult of Devil Worship in America*. New York: Mysterious Press, 1988.

Lyons, A. *The Second Coming; Satanism in America*. New York: Dodd, Mead, 1970.

Mathews, C. *Modern Satanism: Anatomy of a Radical Subculture*. Westport, CT: Praeger, 2009.

McIntosh, C. "Eliphas Lévi." In Christopher Partridge (ed.), *The Occult World*. New York: Routledge, 2015, pp. 220–31.

Melton, J. G. *Encyclopedia of American Religions*. 7th ed. New York: Thomson-Gale, 2003.

Melton, J. G. *The Encyclopedia of Religious Phenomena*. Detroit, MI: Visible Ink, 2008.

Miller, D. "Beyond The Iron Gates: How Nazi-Satanists Infiltrated the UK Underground. *The Quietus* (November 27, 2018). https://goo.by/rkhegR.

Monette, C. R. *Mysticism in the 21st Century*. Wilsonville, OR: Sirius Academic Press, 2013.

Moody, E. J. "Magical Therapy: An Anthropological Investigation of Contemporary Satanism." In I. I. Zaretsky and M. P. Leone (eds.), *Religious Movements in Contemporary America*. Princeton, NJ: Princeton University Press, 1974, pp. 355–82.

Mostrous, A. "The Hampstead Sex Cult Hoax." *Daily Mail* (September 23, 2022). https://goo.by/tNnDRp.

Nathan, D. *Sybil Exposed: The Extraordinary Story behind the Famous Multiple Personality Case*. New York: Free Press, 2011.

Nathan, D., and M. R Snedeker. *Satan's Silence: Ritual Abuse and the Making of a Modern American Witch Hunt*. New York: Basic Books, 1995.

Noblitt, J. T., and P. P. Noblitt, *Cult and Ritual Abuse: Narratives Evidence and Healing Approaches*. 3rd ed. Santa Barbara, CA: Praeger, 2014.

Noll, R. "Speak, Memory." *Psychiatric Times* (March 19, 2014). www.psychiatrictimes.com/view/speak-memory.

Norris, J., and J. A. Potter. "The Devil Made Me Do It." *Penthouse* (January 1986), 50.

Patterson, M. "Satanists Planning Christmas Eve Display in Oklahoma City." *NewsOK.com* (December 11, 2015). goo.by/zBjYBl.

Pennink, E. "Social Media Giants under Pressure over Satanist Linked to Wembley Murders." *Evening Standard* (October 20, 2021). goo.by/eNrYza.

Petersen, J. A. "Contemporary Satanism." In C. Partridge (ed.), *The Occult World*. New York: Routledge, 2015, pp. 396–406.

Petersen, J. A. "Introduction: Embracing Satan." In J. A. Petersen (ed.), *Contemporary Religious Satanism: A Critical Anthology*. Farnham: Ashgate, 2009, pp. 1–24.

Petersen, J. A. "Modern Satanism: Dark Doctrines and Black Flames." In J. R. Lewis and J. A. Petersen (eds.), *Controversial New Religions*. New York: Oxford, 2014, pp. 423–57.

Petersen, J. A. "'Smite Him Hip and Thigh': Satanism, Violence, and Transgression." In J. R. Lewis (ed.), *Violence and New Religious Movements*. New York: Oxford University Press, 2011, pp. 351–78.

Popichak, J. "DA: Man Angered by 'After School Satan Club' Said He'd 'Shoot Everybody.'" *Saucon Source* (February 28, 2013). https://goo.by/LSZYVE.

"Protest and Prayer Fill Air outside Greater Church of Lucifer." *ABC13.com* (October 30, 2015). https://goo.by/XwetZC.

Ramadan, L. "Two Boca Raton Schools Become Battle Ground for Religious Debate." *Palm Beach Post* (January 4, 2017). https://goo.by/GxcLbv.

Reichert, J., and J. T. Richardson. "Decline of a Moral Panic: A Psychological and Socio-legal Examination of the Current Status of Satanism." *Nova Religio* 16.2 (2012), 47–63.

Reinhold, R. "The Longest Trial – A Post-Mortem. Collapse of Child-Abuse Case: So Much Agony for So Little." *New York Times* (January 24, 1990). https://goo.by/NQHzfl.

Rhodes H. T. F. *The Satanic Mass: A Sociological and Criminological Study*. 1st American ed. Secaucus, NJ: Citadel Press, 1954.

Roberts, S. *Witches U.S.A.* New York: Dell, 1971.

Russell, J. "Army Soldier Who Plotted Unit Ambush with Satanic Neo-Nazi Cult Sentenced to 45 Years." *Courthouse News Service* (March 3, 2013). https://goo.by/UczIsL.

"Satanic Rites for Sailor." *Capital Journal* (December 12, 1967), 20.

"Satanic Temple Suit over Boston Council Prayer Moves Forward." *Associated Press* (July 23, 2021). https://goo.by/RnMjTO.

Schock, P. A. *Romantic Satanism: Myth and the Historical Moment in Blake, Shelley, and Byron*. New York: Palgrave Macmillan, 2003.

Schreck, N. *The Satanic Screen: An Illustrated Guide to the Devil in Cinema*. London: Creation, 2001.

Selzer, J. "Twin Temple Are the Satanic Doo-wop Duo Metal Fans Have Embraced." *Loudersound.com* (December 18, 2020). https://goo.by/KIdcDa.

Senholt, J. C. "The Sinister Tradition: Political Esotericism and the Convergence of Radical Islam, Satanism, and National Socialism in the Order of Nine Angles." Master's Thesis, University of Amsterdam, 2009.

Shelley, P. B. *A Defense of Poetry.* Charleston, SC: BiblioLife, 2009.

Sieg, G. "Angular Momentum: From Traditional to Progressive Satanism in the Order of Nine Angles." *International Journal for the Study of New Religions* 4.2 (2013), 251–82.

Sirikupt, C. "Russia Now Says It Must 'De-Satanize' Ukraine. What?" *The Washington Post* (November 17, 2022). https://goo.by/TusMqr.

Smith, G. A. "About Three-in-Ten U.S. Adults Are Now Religiously Unaffiliated." *Pew Research Center* (December 14, 2021). https://goo.by/kosYoG.

Smith, M., and L. Pazder. *Michelle Remembers.* New York: Pocket Books, 1980.

Snyder, H. N., and M. Sickmund. *Juvenile Offenders and Victims: 2006 National Report.* Washington, DC: Office of Juvenile Justice, 2006.

State of Montana Board of Medical Examiners. "Final Order in the Matter of Bennett Braun: Case No. 2019-MED-95" (January 22, 2021).

Strube, J. "The "Baphomet" of Eliphas Lévi: Its Meaning and Historical Context." *Correspondences* 4 (2016), 37–79.

Truzzi, M. "The Occult Revival As Popular Culture: Some Random Observations on the Old and the Nouveau Witch." *Sociological Quarterly* 13.1 (1972), 16–36.

Upchurch, H. E. "The Iron March Forum and the Evolution of the 'Skull Mask' Neo-Fascist Network." *Combating Terrorism Center Sentinel* 14.10 (December 2021). https://goo.by/Hznwdj.

Van Luijk, R. *Children of Lucifer: The Origins of Modern Religious Satanism.* New York: Oxford University Press, 2016.

Van Luijk, R. "Sex, Science, and Liberty: The Resurrection of Satan in Nineteenth-Century (Counter) Culture." In P. Faxneld and J. A. Petersen (eds.), *The Devil's Party: Satanism in Modernity.* New York: Oxford University Press, 2013, pp. 41–52.

Van Zack, G. "Local Satan Worshippers Get Set." *Daily Nexus* 57.44 (November 12, 1976), 1.

Victor, J. S. "Crime, Moral Panic, and the Occult." In Christopher Partridge (ed.), *The Occult World.* New York: Routledge, 2014, pp. 692–700.

Victor, J. S. "Satanic Cult Rumors As Contemporary Legend." *Western Folklore* 49.1 (1990), 51–81.

Ward, H. H. "Satan Rift Centers in Detroit." *Detroit Free Press* (March 25, 1972), B11.

Warnke, Mike. *The Satan Seller.* Plainfield, NJ: Logos International, 1972.

Winston, A. "Neo-Nazi Satanist Cult Is a Terrorist Group, Feds Say." *Rolling Stone* (July 6, 2022). https://goo.by/sXRlWe.

Woods, R. *The Devil.* Chicago, IL: Thomas More Press, 1974.

Wright, L. *Saints & Sinners: Walker Railey, Jimmy Swaggart, Madalyn Murray O'Hair, Anton LaVey, Will Campbell, Matthew Fox.* New York: Knopf, 1993.

Wright, L. "Sympathy for the Devil: It's Not Easy Being Evil in a World That's Gone to Hell." *Rolling Stone* 612 (1991), 63–8, 105–6.

Cambridge Elements ⁼

New Religious Movements

Founding Editor

†James R. Lewis

Wuhan University

The late James R. Lewis was Professor of Philosophy at Wuhan University, China. He served as the editor or co-editor for four book series, was the general editor for the *Alternative Spirituality and Religion Review*, and the associate editor for the *Journal of Religion and Violence*. His publications include *The Cambridge Companion to Religion and Terrorism* (Cambridge University Press 2017) and *Falun Gong: Spiritual Warfare and Martyrdom* (Cambridge University Press 2018).

Series Editor

Rebecca Moore

San Diego State University

Rebecca Moore is Emerita Professor of Religious Studies at San Diego State University. She has written and edited numerous books and articles on Peoples Temple and the Jonestown tragedy. Publications include *Beyond Brainwashing: Perspectives on Cultic Violence* (Cambridge University Press 2018) and *Peoples Temple and Jonestown in the Twenty-First Century* (Cambridge University Press 2022). She is reviews editor for *Nova Religio*, the quarterly journal on new and emergent religions published by the University of California Press.

About the Series

Elements in New Religious Movements go beyond cult stereotypes and popular prejudices to present new religions and their adherents in a scholarly and engaging manner. Case studies of individual groups, such as Transcendental Meditation and Scientology, provide in-depth consideration of some of the most well known, and controversial, groups. Thematic examinations of women, children, science, technology, and other topics focus on specific issues unique to these groups. Historical analyses locate new religions in specific religious, social, political, and cultural contexts. These examinations demonstrate why some groups exist in tension with the wider society and why others live peaceably in the mainstream. The series highlights the differences, as well as the similarities, within this great variety of religious expressions. To discuss contributing to this series please contact Professor Moore, remoore@sdsu.edu.

Cambridge Elements ⹀

New Religious Movements

Elements in the Series

A full series listing is available at: www.cambridge.org/ENRM

Printed in the United States
by Baker & Taylor Publisher Services